IDIOT'S GUIDES
AS EASY AS IT GETS!

Cooking Basics

by Chef Thomas N. England

ALPHA

A member of Penguin Random House LLC

ALPHA BOOKS

Published by Penguin Random House LLC

Penguin Random House LLC, 375 Hudson Street, New York, New York 10014, USA · Penguin Random House LLC (Canada), 90 Eglinton Avenue East, Suite 700, Toronto, Ontario M4P 2Y3, Canada (a division of Pearson Penguin Canada Inc.) · Penguin Books Ltd., 80 Strand, London WC2R 0RL, England · Penguin Ireland, 25 St. Stephen's Green, Dublin 2, Ireland (a division of Penguin Books Ltd.) · Penguin Random House LLC (Australia), 250 Camberwell Road, Camberwell, Victoria 3124, Australia (a division of Pearson Australia Group Pty. Ltd.) · Penguin Books India Pvt. Ltd., 11 Community Centre, Panchsheel Park, New Delhi—110 017, India · Penguin Random House LLC (NZ), 67 Apollo Drive, Rosedale, North Shore, Auckland 1311, New Zealand (a division of Pearson New Zealand Ltd.) · Penguin Books (South Africa) (Pty.) Ltd., 24 Sturdee Avenue, Rosebank, Johannesburg 2196, South Africa · Penguin Books Ltd., Registered Offices: 80 Strand, London WC2R 0RL, England

001-280242-September2015

IDIOT'S GUIDES and Design are trademarks of Penguin Random House LLC

International Standard Book Number: 978-1-61564-819-1
Library of Congress Catalog Card Number: 2015930787

17 16 15   8 7 6 5 4 3 2 1

Interpretation of the printing code: The rightmost number of the first series of numbers is the year of the book's printing; the rightmost number of the second series of numbers is the number of the book's printing. For example, a printing code of 15-1 shows that the first printing occurred in 2015.

Printed in China

Note: This publication contains the opinions and ideas of its author. It is intended to provide helpful and informative material on the subject matter covered. It is sold with the understanding that the author and publisher are not engaged in rendering professional services in the book. If the reader requires personal assistance or advice, a competent professional should be consulted. The author and publisher specifically disclaim any responsibility for any liability, loss, or risk, personal or otherwise, which is incurred as a consequence, directly or indirectly, of the use and application of any of the contents of this book.

Most Alpha books are available at special quantity discounts for bulk purchases for sales promotions, premiums, fund-raising, or educational use. Special books, or book excerpts, can also be created to fit specific needs. For details, write: Special Markets, Alpha Books, 375 Hudson Street, New York, NY 10014.

Trademarks: All terms mentioned in this book that are known to be or are suspected of being trademarks or service marks have been appropriately capitalized. Alpha Books and Penguin Random House LLC cannot attest to the accuracy of this information. Use of a term in this book should not be regarded as affecting the validity of any trademark or service mark.

PUBLISHER:
Mike Sanders

ASSOCIATE PUBLISHER:
Billy Fields

SENIOR ACQUISITIONS EDITOR:
Brook Farling

DEVELOPMENT EDITOR:
John Etchison

COVER AND BOOK DESIGNER:
Rebecca Batchelor

PRODUCTION EDITOR:
Jana M. Stefanciosa

INDEXER:
Celia McCoy

PREPRESS:
Brian Massey

PROOFREADER:
Virginia Vasquez Vought

PHOTOGRAPHER:
Gabrielle Cheikh Photography

Contents

salads 107

beef and pork 125

poultry 147

seafood 165

pastas and grains . . . 187

potatoes and beans 209

fruits and vegetables 227

Index 258

Introduction

I've been teaching basic cooking classes for 10 years, and during that time I've seen great changes in the ways people think about cooking. Not too long ago, meals were largely consumed outside the home and treated more as convenience foods. Today, people are headed back into the kitchen to once again enjoy making meals that are healthier and made from scratch, and sharing them with friends and family. This evolution has created a need for new cooks to understand basic cooking techniques.

This book was written especially to help the inexperienced cook get off to a good start in the kitchen. The first chapter explains the basics of setting up a well-stocked, organized, and safe kitchen, and then defines some terminology and techniques the new cook will encounter in this book. The subsequent chapters begin with important general information about each food group and explain how they're raised or grown, where and how to buy them, and how to store them safely. Each chapter then contains delicious recipes for some of the most common dishes for each food group.

The recipes presented in these pages are building blocks you can use to be creative while developing your own kitchen repertoire. I teach you how to use different ingredients and methods to make variations of many of the dishes, so as you practice and grow, you can come up with your own variations.

Learning basic cooking skills is not as complicated as you might think. This book teaches you the fundamentals you'll need to know and use throughout your cooking experiences. With this foundation you can enjoy creating and sharing glorious meals that start with making the easy recipes contained in this book.

Acknowledgments

There are several people I would like to thank for their help. Without their guidance and support, it would not have been possible for me to write this book.

First of all, thank you to Karen Mangia for her constant love, support, and patience. She is the person who's ever present to encourage me and make sure that all my needs are taken care of. When writing deadlines were due during the busy holiday season, Karen stepped up and made the holidays happen as usual.

A special thank you to Donna Bricker, who helped produce and arrange the foods for the pictures in this book. With hundreds of pictures taken, Donna always made sure every piece of onion was where it belonged.

Writing is truly a team effort. A huge thank you to the team at Alpha Books who make these words seem effortless. The team of editors who have scoured the book and art editors who make it look good are the people who really made this book happen.

My mother and brother, Joanna and Tony England, are the reason I followed my passion for food and drink. They have always encouraged me to follow my nose.

the basics

In this chapter, you'll learn all the basics
of the kitchen. From recipe terminology
to basic equipment to safety precautions
to take while working in the kitchen—it's
all covered. It's recommended that you
read this chapter before moving further
into cooking.

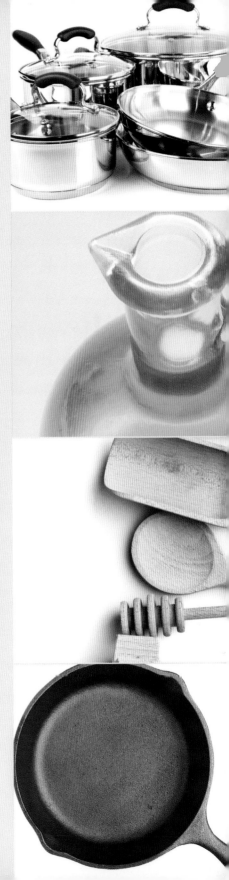

The Fundamentals of Cooking

My years of teaching basic cooking classes have given me a good understanding of what inexperienced cooks want to know when they're beginning to learn to cook. The knowledge any aspiring cook needs can be narrowed down to the following few categories:

1. **Understand what fundamental cooking terms mean.** This was illustrated very well when a student told me she was in a grocery store for an hour looking for the "roux" called for in a recipe. She didn't realize roux is simply flour and fat cooked together to make a thickener.

2. **Know what you need before you start cooking.** I was invited to attend a dinner party one evening, and the host had not read through his recipes entirely. Little did he realize that one of the recipes called for the food to marinate for two hours before it was cooked—or that the recipe called for basic pantry items he did not have. It was after midnight when we finally sat down to the entrée.

3. **Know proper weights, measures, and ratios.** I once was judging a cookie baking competition on live television when I bit into a chocolate chip cookie that had baking soda measured in tablespoons instead of teaspoons. Needless to say, a cookie baked with three times the amount of baking soda called for can elicit a pretty sour face for the camera. Using the correct measurements makes the difference between a delicious creation and a total disaster.

4. **Always be sure to work safely in the kitchen.** Safety should be the primary concern in any kitchen, private or commercial. You're always working with potentially hazardous foods, sharp knives, and burning hot stoves and pots. Without a basic knowledge of safely handling these dangers, you or someone you cook for could become injured or very sick.

You will learn all of these important fundamentals in this chapter. You may need to return to this foundation many times as you learn to cook. You can use this chapter as a reference to look up the definitions of important terms, purchase necessary supplies for your pantry, understand the proper use of tools, and find the right cookware and equipment for your kitchen.

Cooking Terminology

The art of cooking has a language of its own. This list is an introduction to the different cooking techniques and actions you can perform in your kitchen.

al dente   An Italian term that means "to the tooth"—cooked until there is some firmness, but not crunchy.

au jus   The oil-free liquid that comes out of meat when it's roasted, and is used as a sauce.

balsamic vinegar   A dark, sweet vinegar originally produced in Italy from a specific variety of grape and aged in wooden barrels.

barbeque   To cook at a low temperature with smoke.

baste   To take the oils that collect in the bottom of a roasting pan while cooking meat and pour them back over the top of the meat.

béchamel   A basic sauce that contains dairy and a thickener. It's a mother sauce that's used to make many other sauces.

blanch   To boil in water for a short amount of time without fully cooking the item.

brown   To change the natural sugars in the food to a brown color using dry heat cooking.

caramelize   To change the natural sugars in the food to a brown color using dry heat cooking.

dash   A liquid measurement equal to $\frac{1}{8}$ of a teaspoon.

deglaze   To collect the pan drippings from cooking by adding a liquid to the pan and stirring.

dredge   To coat the food with a liquid or flour.

emulsify   To whisk a liquid such as oil in a way that binds the liquid and fat molecules to each other.

glaze   To add a thin layer of liquid over the entire surface of a food.

julienne   A food that is cut exactly to $\frac{1}{8}$ by $\frac{1}{8}$ by 2 inches (.5cm by .5cm by 5cm).

marinate   To allow a food to set in an acidic flavorful liquid in order to enrich the end flavor.

on-the-bias   To slice an item at a 45-degree angle or more rather than a straight cut.

poach   To cook in a liquid that is between 160°F (71°C) and 180°F (82°C).

preheat   To heat an oven or pan before the food is placed in it.

purée   To turn a semi-solid food into a thick, creamy liquid, usually with a blender.

reduce   To simmer a liquid and allow the water to evaporate.

remoulade A sauce that contains mayonnaise, chopped pickles, herbs, and other flavorings; similar to tartar sauce.

render To sauté an item that has fat in it until the oils come out.

rest To allow a cooked food to sit in a warm, but not hot, place so the internal juices distribute evenly. Meat that is not allowed to rest before cutting will likely be dry,

roux The basic thickener used in classical cooking, made of equal parts fat and flour cooked together.

sachet d'épices A tied bundle made of cheesecloth containing bay leaf, thyme, parsley stems, garlic, and black peppercorns. It's the classic seasoning combination used in European-based cooking.

sauté To cook at a high temperature in a sauté pan with very little oil.

scale To measure using weight.

score To cut a shallow slit in something without cutting through it.

sear To sauté to allow caramelization to occur $1/4$ inch (.5cm) into the food.

shred To use a shredder to cut into small pieces.

simmer To cook a liquid at a temperature of 180°F to 210°F (82° and 99°C).

stir-fry To cook in a pan or wok that is very hot. This process cooks the outside of the food but leaves the inside warm and preserves more of the nutrients.

stock A flavorful liquid made by cooking meats and/or vegetables with seasonings and then straining to remove the solids and leave the liquid. Stock is often used as a base for soups and stews.

sweat To cook in a sauté pan on low to medium heat without causing caramelization in the food.

velouté A thickened white stock that's used as the base for many sauces and soups.

whisk To stir a liquid using a wire tool, which is also called a whisk.

zest To remove very thin strips of the outside of a citrus fruit with a special tool called a zester. The more white rind in the zest, the more bitter the taste.

Basic Kitchen Tools

This list includes tools every kitchen should have on hand. It's recommended that you go to a restaurant supply store to purchase these items instead of a department or grocery store. In most cases, the items are of better quality and are less expensive, and most restaurant supply stores are open to the public and will be happy to assist you with purchasing decisions.

kitchen fork   A 2-pronged meat fork.

offset spatula   Sometimes called a "hamburger turner" or "pancake turner."

high-temperature rubber spatula   A spatula made with silicone rubber to withstand high heat. They're great to use interchangeably with a wooden spoon.

wooden spoons   Always nice to have around to mix and stir with. Look for spoons that have a square bowl, which makes it easier to scrape the bottom of a pot.

whisk   Look for one that has the most wire loops and is the right size for what you plan to do with it.

scale   The digital type is the best choice. Make sure it will weigh tenths of an ounce.

kitchen fork

offset spatula

rubber spatula

wooden spoon

whisk

scale

ladle

measuring cups

measuring spoons

instant-read thermometer

pots

sauté pan

sauce pan

cast iron pan

ladle   The 2-ounce (60mL), 4-ounce (120mL), and 8-ounce (240mL) sizes are all handy to have.

measuring cups   The narrower cups are easier to work with than wider ones.

measuring spoons   Metal spoons with deeper cavities work the best.

instant-read thermometer   The digital type will read faster than the dials. Make sure it has a function that allows you to calibrate. Also, look for a temperature range that goes from 32°F (0°C) to at least 450°F (232°C).

in-oven thermometer   This is a thermometer you can leave inside food placed in the oven, with a wire that leads out of the oven to a control that tells the actual temperature.

pots   Several sizes are nice to have: you should have a 1-quart (1L), 2-quart (2L), and 4-quart (4L) as well as a 2-gallon (7.5L) pot in the kitchen. Look for stainless steel pots with heavy bottoms. Do not get nonstick.

sauté pans   These should have curved edges, not straight. You should have at least three different sizes. Look for stainless steel pans with a heavy bottom. Do not get nonstick; if the proper cooking techniques are used, food won't stick to stainless steel.

sauce pan   Pans with straight sides. Two different sizes are good to have.

cast iron pan   Every household should have at least one of these that's 10 to 12 inches (25.5 to 30.5cm) at the base. If treated with care, it can be handed down for many generations.

sheet pan   This should be no more than $^1/_2$ inch (1.25cm) tall at the sides, and a thick type is better. If it's too thin, it will buckle and bend in a hot oven.

rack   Sometimes referred to as a cooling rack, this rack should fit into your sheet pan for better roasting.

strainer   A bowl-shaped screen, often with a handle. This is used to separate liquids from solids.

food processor   A machine used to cut, purée, chop, or shred.

blender   A stand-up pitcher with blades in the bottom that fits onto a motor. The type often found in bars is ideal. The motor and gears should be heavy duty.

mixer   Stand mixers are preferred over hand mixers as they will mix more evenly.

hand blender   This type of blender can be put directly into a pot of liquid and used to purée. It's much cleaner and easier than using a bar-style blender for hot foods.

sheet pan

rack

strainer

food processor

blender

mixer

hand blender

Caring for Cast Iron and Sauté Pans

Cast iron pans and sauté pans should be treated in the same way. There is some mystique around cast iron that it needs to be treated differently, while in fact all pans should be treated specially.

To season your pans, heat them on a burner until they start to smoke, then rub them with cooking oil that's been applied to a cloth. Repeat this process three times.

After each use, clean the pan under running water with a scratch pad. Do not use soap—you'll find the pan wipes clean pretty easily. After the pan is clean, immediately dry it by putting it back on the stove and heating it until all the water is evaporated. Never allow pans to sit with liquid in them, as they will rust or pit.

This is the same process you would use with "nonstick" pans. Even with those, you should never use soap to clean.

Proper Measuring

Measurements for cooking and baking are based on either volume or weight. Volume measurement is done with measuring cups and spoons, or with a graduated cup. Weight is measured using a scale.

When using a **measuring cup** or **spoon,** mound the item being measured in the cup or spoon and run the flat edge of a knife across the top to level the product. That's considered a level measure.

If you're using a **graduated cup** or **pitcher,** keep in mind these are less accurate. To get a true measure, put the product being measured in the cup and make sure it's level at the point where you're measuring. Put it on a level surface and bend down to look at the measure at eye level. If the surface is not level it will be lower at one side, and won't be accurate. If you're looking down at the measure, it will look like it's at a higher level than it actually is.

The first step in using a **scale** to measure is to figure the *tare* weight. This means putting the empty container that will hold the ingredient on the scale first, and setting the scale to zero. You can then measure the weight by adding the product to the container.

 Measuring Fluid Ounces
Keep in mind whether a recipe calls for *fluid* ounces, which is a volume measure and different from a weight measure. If you weigh 1 cup of flour, you'll notice it weighs only about 4 ounces (120mL). It's a common misconception that 1 cup is always 8 ounces (240mL). This is only true for liquids with the density of water.

Yields and Measures

3 teaspoons = 1 tablespoon

16 tablespoons = 1 cup

2 cups = 1 pint (480mL)

2 pints = 1 quart (1L)

4 quarts = 1 gallon

1 dash = less than $^1/_8$ teaspoon

1 teaspoon = $^1/_6$ fluid ounce (6.25mL)

1 tablespoon = $^1/_2$ fluid ounce (12.5mL)

1 cup = 8 fluid ounces (240mL)

1 pint = 16 fluid ounces (470mL)

1 quart = 32 fluid ounces (1L)

1 gallon = 128 fluid ounces (4L)

1 peck = 2 gallons

1 bushel = 4 pecks

Freezing point = 32°F (0°C)

Boiling point = 212°F (100°C)

Setting Up a Pantry

Following are some items you should stock in your cabinets, refrigerator, or freezer when you start setting up your kitchen.

Condiments

Ketchup   The better ketchups will be higher in tomato content and lower in sugar and sodium. These have an indefinite shelf life.

Mustard   There are lots of varieties to choose from, from grainy to spicy, and from brown to electric yellow. These also have an indefinite shelf life.

Salsa   The most popular condiment in many cultures. Pico de Gallo style salsa is a staple. These can be homemade or store bought.

Mayonnaise   Look for versions with the fewest ingredients. You can also make your own.

Hot chile sauce   A hot sauce made from chile peppers, often referred to as Tabasco sauce.

Dairy

Milk   Milk is most often classified by fat content. When drinking milk, most people consume lower fat versions (no-fat, skim milk), but when cooking, the fats are necessary for chemical reactions. Whole (vitamin D) milk is preferred for cooking. If you cook with low-fat milks, remember that the sugar levels are higher and you'll need to adjust the heat in order to avoid burning the sugars.

Heavy cream   Heavy cream and heavy whipping cream are considered the same for cooking purposes. These are higher in fat content which helps with the cooking process, and they both emulsify with water to make things thicker.

Sour cream   Sour cream is milk with a higher acidity level, causing the curd to become firm yet spreadable. This condiment is used in many foods for the acid balance it adds.

Cheese   Cheeses come in many unique varieties, each based on firmness, aging, and what molds are present. Lactose-intolerant people can enjoy aged cheeses because as a cheese ages, the lactose sugars are converted to acids.

Other Necessities

Flour　There are three main types of flour, based on the amount of proteins (glutens) they contain. The highest-gluten flour is bread flour. The glutens help to build the structure in breads that trap air pockets. Cake flour is the lowest in gluten. When making a cake, you don't want the big air bubbles being trapped in gluten. All-purpose flour balances bread flour and cake flour so the glutens are in between the two and is the main flour you should keep in your kitchen.

Vinegars　Vinegars are acidified alcohols. The main three that should be kept in your cabinet are red wine, white wine, and apple cider vinegars.

Oils　Oils are fats from nuts and seeds. They're categorized by what they come from, whether they're cold pressed, and whether they're filtered. In general, if you're going to consume an oil without cooking it you'll want cold pressed and unfiltered for the best flavor. If you're cooking with it, you'll want something that has less flavor as the purpose of the oil is to transport heat and not to add a lot of flavor. Many people cook only with extra virgin olive oil, but in reality, this oil doesn't do well at high heat and will add a lot of bad flavors to the food. The other thing to take into consideration with cooking oils is the *smoke point*. This is the point at which the oils start to deteriorate and smoke. The best for sautéing are the higher smoke point oils.

Smoke Points of Common Oils and Fats

Whole butter	350°F (176°C)
Clarified butter	485°F (251°C)
Vegetable oil	400°F (204°C)
Corn oil	450°F (232°C)
Grape seed oil	485°F (251°C)
Extra virgin olive oil	375°F (190°C)
Olive oil, not extra virgin	465°F (240°C)
Peanut oil	450°F (232°C)

Standard Produce

There is some commonly used produce that's good to always have available in the kitchen.

Carrots   These root vegetables will stay fresh in the refrigerator for six months.

Onions   Three main types of onions are common: white, yellow, and sweet.

The white onion is often used in Mexican foods, and has an assertive, spicy quality.

Yellow onions are the most commonly used. You should keep a bag of these in your pantry; they will last up to 9 months without going bad.

Sweet onions are just that—sweet. Because of their high sugar content, they do not store well.

Celery   Celery is high in nitrates, which is a natural preservative, so it can be kept in the refrigerator for several months.

Garlic   Garlic is a staple in many types of cooking, and can be stored for up to an entire year in the pantry. Note that garlic powder does not take the place of fresh garlic.

Herbs and Spices

Cooking with herbs and spices elevates a mundane dish into an aromatic dream. A basic broth is transformed into a mouthwatering soup with the delicate addition of salt, thyme, pepper, parsley, and bay leaf. Zucchini would be nothing without the healthy addition of fresh basil. The smell of chicken roasting in the oven would not make you as hungry without the aromas of the herbs roasting with it.

Herbs and spices line a rack or cabinet in nearly every home. The combinations often can give clues to heritage, ethnicity, and even religion of the chef. Because herbs and spices are so important in the development of the base smells of the food we cook, special care needs to be taken to ensure the best flavors.

Herbs

Herbs are flavorful edible leaves, and when fresh, they have bright, clean aromas. To store fresh herbs, remove them from any plastic packaging, wrap them in a wet paper towel, and place them in a refrigerator crisper drawer. They'll stay fresh for up to two weeks. Unfortunately, fresh herbs aren't always available, so if you have to use dried herbs, make sure they're no more than six months old or the flavors will be diminished. It's a good idea to mark the purchase dates on the containers you store them in, and make sure the containers are airtight. Dried herbs are a concentrated version of the herb; therefore, if you substitute dried for fresh herbs, use one fourth of the amount stated in the recipe.

 Chef's Note

Many of the recipes in this book call for a *sachet d'épices*, a combination of herbs and spices tied together in a square of cheesecloth. The ingredients typically include bay leaf, thyme, peppercorn, parsley stems, and garlic cloves. The sachet d'épices is added to soups and stocks for flavor and removed before serving.

Bay leaf   This leaf of the bay laurel tree is one of the most common ingredients in a sachet d'épices. Bay leaf is used in the base for cooking soups, stocks, and stews. It's added to liquids as a whole leaf and removed before serving.

Chives   A delicate member of the onion family, chives are used on eggs, chicken, potatoes, fish, and shellfish.

Cilantro   A strong and citrusy herb, the leaf of this plant is used in many Asian, Mexican, and South American dishes.

Dill   Thin, feathery leaves make dill very distinctive. This herb has aromas of anise and black licorice. It's common in Scandinavian cooking and often used with eggs and fish.

Mint   This herb has a very strong and distinctive menthol flavor. It usually is not used with other herbs because it easily overpowers them. Mint is often used with chocolate.

Oregano   A pungent pepper quality is noticeable in oregano. It's often used in Mediterranean cuisines, and is the classic accompaniment to tomatoes.

Parsley   This is the most widely used herb in the world, and it grows well in almost every climate. Parsley has a tangy yet clean flavor.

Rosemary   This is an evergreen plant that grows in hot, dry climates. The needles add a pine-like flavor to foods. Rosemary pairs particularly well with lamb.

Sage   This herb has strong balsamic and camphor scents, and doesn't work well with other herbs. It's best used with poultry dishes or brewed into a tea.

Tarragon   The long leaves of this plant are often chopped and used in sauces. It has a strong flavor of anise or licorice.

Thyme   This is a strong herb that plays well with others. Some people say the smell is like sage, but more refined. Thyme is also a common ingredient in a sachet d'épices.

Spices

Spices are the seeds, bark, or roots of plants. Spices have a long history of use dating back to the Egyptians in 2800 B.C.E. Their use was a sign of luxury and they came with high prices even into the nineteenth century. Historically, the plants that spices were derived from came mainly from Indonesia. Now, spice plants are cultivated in many other countries, which has helped bring prices down.

Spices can come in whole form, but most often are powdered. Whole spices are ground into a recipe as needed, a technique that brings the richest flavors to the dish. Whole spices can maintain their quality for two years in an airtight container. Once they're powdered they begin to lose flavor, and should be disposed of after six months.

Cayenne   Ground hot red chile peppers that are used more for spicy heat than for flavor.

Chili powder   This is a combination of chile peppers ground with oregano, cumin, garlic, and other seasonings.

Cinnamon   This popular spice comes from the bark of a type of evergreen tree. It's most often associated with pastries, but is also a great pairing for lamb dishes and stews.

Clove   Cloves are the unopened buds of a type of evergreen tree. They have a sweet aroma and are very astringent.

Coriander   This has a sweet, spicy flavor with a strong aroma. Though coriander is the seed of the cilantro plant, the two cannot be used interchangeably because their flavors are so different.

Cumin   Cumin has a strong earthy flavor, and is often used in Indian and Mexican foods.

Ginger   This is a rhizome of a tropical plant. A group of fingerlike nodules growing together is called a "hand." Ginger has a spicy but sweet flavor that is used in most Asian cuisines. The scent resembles citrus and rosemary.

Mustard (dried)   Mustard comes from plants in the cabbage family. It's used in pickling and as the main component in the condiment.

Pepper   This is the main spice used for seasoning. It adds a spicy note to foods without overpowering them.

Types of Peppercorns

Green	Fruit is picked before it's fully ripened.	Mild flavor.
Black	Fruit is picked ripe and dehydrated.	Pungent, hot flavor.
White	Fruit is picked ripe and dehydrated; outer layers are processed off.	Pungent, somewhat hot, more floral character than black.
Pink	Completely different plant than the other three.	Sweet with aromas of roses.

Salts

Salt is another ingredient with a long history and at one time was even used as currency. Salt preserves food, takes flavors to new heights, and adds a distinctive taste. Almost every recipe has salt in the ingredients list, yet little thought is given to which salt is best. Salt is most often used in recipes to help with a chemical reaction in the cooking process, which means it needs to be unaltered. If a recipe calls for salt, it's best to use kosher or sea salt for all around cooking; iodized salt is more compact and is not hollow like kosher and sea salt because its cell structure is altered when iodine is added. It also cannot absorb water as easily and the cooking is slowed down when water is present. Sea salts also contain higher levels of minerals, which impart unique flavors. Salt is the most commonly used pantry item.

Types of Salt

Table salt	Very dense mined salt, mostly from New York. Often other chemicals such as iodine and anti-caking agents are added. This is most often used in salt shakers. It's good for baking applications, but should rarely be used for meat preparation.
Kosher salt	Can come from the earth or the sea. It dissolves easily and has a looser cell structure than table salt. This is a good all-purpose salt. It gets its name from its use in kosher meat preparation, though not all kosher salt is certified kosher.
Fleur de sel	Sea salt that has been harvested from evaporating ponds as the salt forms on top of the water. Use this salt on foods after they've been cooked.
Sel gris/grey salt	Salt collected from the bottom of evaporating ponds. This salt contains minerals from the sea. It's ideal for cooking fatty meats and root vegetables.
Hawaiian sea salt	These salts can be either pink or black. The pink color comes from the red clay soils around the islands, and the black comes from volcanic ash. This salt is ideal for pork and seafood.
Himalayan salt	This salt is mined from deposits in Pakistan, and is said to be the purest form of salt. It's often counterfeited by adding red color. Finer grinds are great for general use.

Knives

The most used tool in any kitchen is a knife. It's imperative that you know how to use knives properly and that you maintain a sharp edge on all the knives you own. Buying high-quality knives made from forged steel will help you keep the blades sharp for easy, efficient work.

The Most Important Knives

There are three types of knives that no kitchen should be without.

1 The **chef's knife** or **French knife.** This is by far the most used knife in a kitchen. It's 8 to 14 inches (20.5 to 35.5cm) long, with a handle offset from the blade so you can put the sharp side down without hitting your knuckles on the table.

2 The **paring knife.** This knife is smaller so you can do fine detail work when the chef's knife is too big. Unfortunately, this is the knife beginning cooks gravitate toward. Don't do it—this is also the knife people more often cut themselves with because they're using it for the wrong tasks.

3 The **serrated slicing knife.** This knife is ideal for cutting breads. The serrations help catch and slice the bread without compressing it. It can be used for slicing meats, but will leave ridges on the surface of the meat.

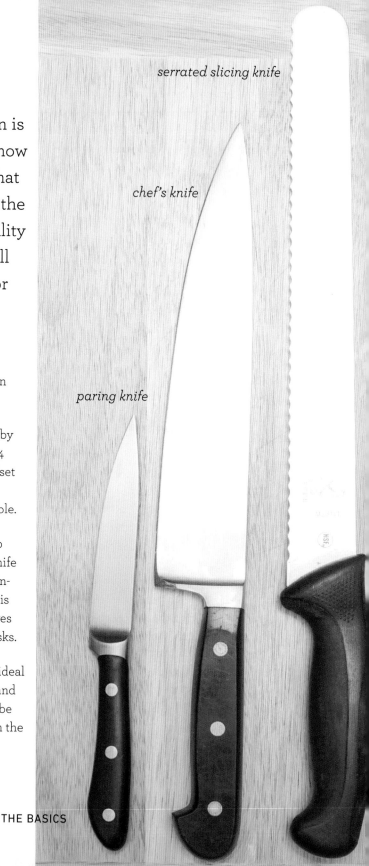

serrated slicing knife

chef's knife

paring knife

Knife Construction

A knife is made up of the blade, the bolster, and the handle.

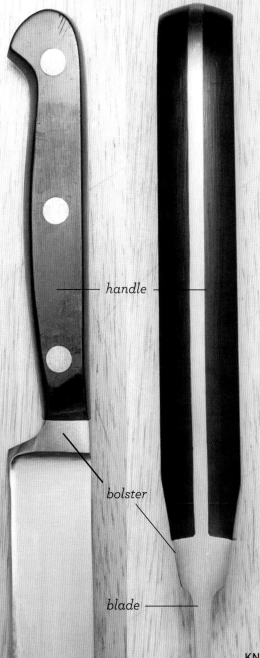

handle

bolster

blade

The **blade** should be made of high-carbon steel, which holds a sharp edge longer and doesn't corrode. The metal of the blade should extend all the way through the handle, as well. This is called a "full tang" blade. If it only sticks part way into the handle it's called a "half tang" blade.

The **bolster** is the point where the sharp part of the blade stops and transitions into the handle. High-quality knives are balanced at this point. You should be able to rest the bolster on the tip of your finger and the knife will stay level. This is also the point where you'll grip the blade. Good balance means you won't have to work as hard when cutting with the knife.

The **handle** should be a size that fits your hand well. Some handles are wider and some are smaller. Look for the size that feels most comfortable in your hand—you'll be using your knives a lot.

Holding a Knife
When you hold a knife, the index finger and the thumb should be on either side of the bolster gripping the blade. Your other three fingers should drape around the handle. The control of the knife is really just in the index finger and thumb.

Knife Skills

Good knife skills are required for many tasks in the kitchen, including cutting foods into pieces that are the same size. This is important because different size pieces will cook at different rates, so some might end up over-cooked and others undercooked.

Common Knife Cuts

Slicing

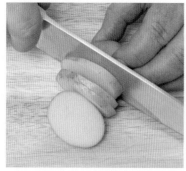

Square off the edges of the item.

Batonnet ($\frac{1}{4}$ × $\frac{1}{4}$ × 2 inches; .5 × .5 × 5cm) and *julienne* ($\frac{1}{8}$ × $\frac{1}{8}$ × 2 inches; 3mm × 3mm × 5cm) are similar in steps when cutting.

Cut into 2-inch (5cm) lengths.

Cut the 2-inch (5cm) lengths into slices of the desired width: $\frac{1}{4}$ inch (.5cm) or $\frac{1}{8}$ inch (3mm).

Cut the flats into a matchstick shape of the desired width: $\frac{1}{4}$ inch (.5cm) or $\frac{1}{8}$ inch (3mm).

Large dice ($^3/_4$ × $^3/_4$ × $^3/_4$ inch; 2 × 2 × 2cm), *medium dice* ($^1/_2$ × $^1/_2$ × $^1/_2$ inch; 1.25 × 1.25 × 1.25cm), and *small dice* ($^1/_4$ × $^1/_4$ × $^1/_4$ inch; .5 × .5 × .5cm) all start the same as the batonnet or julienne. Then they're cut one last time across the matchstick shape to produce cubes that are perfectly diced.

Mince is not an exact cut. It uses the same steps as a dice, but is smaller and less uniform.

Chop is when an herb, vegetable, or other item is sliced through randomly over and over again to make small bits.

Chiffonade is the process of stacking several leaves together, rolling them, and slicing them into consistent threads. This is done with herbs and leafy vegetables.

Place herb leaves on top of one another and roll them tightly.

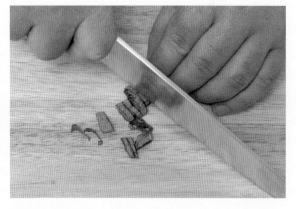

Slice through the rolled leaves evenly to cut uniform sizes.

 Chef's Tip

To cut on a bias is to slice something at a 45-degree angle. This allows you to see more of the item being cut when it's put flat on the plate.

Sharpening a Knife

Maintaining a sharp edge on your knives is very important. Not only are you more likely to cut yourself by struggling to slice through things by applying excessive force to a dull knife, but you also won't be able to make the precise cuts that a sharp knife provides.

I highly recommend that you have your knives sharpened by a kitchen knife sharpening professional on at least a yearly basis, it's the best way to get a precision edge. In between those times, however, you can still easily keep a sharp edge on your knives at home by using a sharpening stone and a steel. The steel helps to develop a final honed edge to the knife. It will not sharpen a dull knife, only fine-tune a sharp one.

Using a sharpening stone

 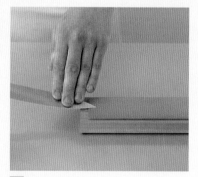 

1 Place the stone on a flat, level surface and put a thin layer of honing oil on the stone. Tilt the knife so the blade is at a 20-degree angle.

2 Pull the knife across the stone to run the whole length of the knife over the stone; be sure to maintain a 20-degree angle the entire way.

3 Turn the knife over. Repeat steps 1 and 2 three times to sharpen the opposite side.

Using a sharpening steel

1 Place the steel on top of a cutting board or folded towel so that the tip of the steel is the only thing touching the board. Hold the handle of the steel at the top using your non-dominant hand. Place the edge of the knife where the bolster meets the blade, near the top of the metal of the steel and just below the handle.

2 Make sure the knife is at a 20-degree angle to the steel. Run the length of the blade down the steel while maintaining the 20-degree angle.

3 Move the knife to the opposite side of the steel to hone the other side of the blade. Repeat steps 2 and 3 three times to finish sharpening your knife.

Kitchen and Food Safety

When you're working in the kitchen, there are a lot of things to be concerned about besides burning your dinner. Always remember that you're working with fire, burning hot objects, sharp utensils, and potentially harmful foods. As you're balancing all these things, keep in mind the following safety precautions.

Food Storage

Any foods that could be potentially hazardous should be kept below 40°F (4.5°C) or above 140°F (60°C). Everything in between is the danger zone. If a food item is in this danger zone for more than four hours, it should be thrown out.

When storing food in the refrigerator, think about what's on the shelves below in case something drips from one shelf to a lower one. You don't want raw chicken juices dripping into a bag of lettuce that will not be cooked.

Cross Contamination

Cross contamination is the biggest danger in the kitchen. This can occur when you're working with one item and then touch something else and contaminate it with bacteria from the first item. This can happen in many ways. You could be cutting chicken and then turn on the water to wash your hands. After your hands are clean, you turn off the tap and get some unsuspected bacteria back on your hands from when you turned the water on. You then dry your hands on a towel that's been used over and over again. Each time you use that towel, you spread the bacteria somewhere else. This is just one example, so be very cautious about what you and the food touch.

 Chef's Note

Recent studies have shown the average household refrigerator temperature is commonly above 45°F (7°C). This was even true when the refrigerator had a temperature control dial. It's important to have a calibrated thermometer you can put in the refrigerator to make sure your food is not being stored within the danger zone.

Personal Safety

Always know who and what's around you before you make any moves. Walking backward is a big problem in the kitchen, as you can't see if you're walking into someone holding a knife or a hot pan. And if you walk behind someone, make sure to announce "Behind you" so they don't turn into you.

Even with precautions, accidents happen. Keep a well-stocked first aid kit and a fire extinguisher in your kitchen where they're easily accessible.

Using a Meat Thermometer

It's common practice for home cooks to cook by time rather than by temperature. A recipe might say to cook a meat 45 minutes or until done, so the cook lets the meat cook for 45 minutes but never checks the internal temperature which could mean it may be way overcooked or very undercooked. Always check meats with a thermometer to make sure they're thoroughly cooked, and remove them from the oven before they're overcooked.

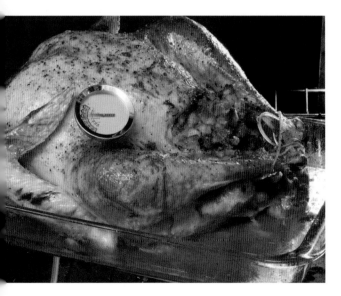

USDA Recommended Cooking Temperatures

Beef, pork, veal, lamb, fish, game steaks, and roasts	145°F (63°C)
Ground meats	160°F (71°C)
Ham and bacon	155°F (68°C)
Poultry	165°F (74°C)

Cooking Techniques

There are eight basic cooking techniques: sautéing, grilling, frying, boiling, steaming, simmering, poaching, and braising. Once you understand the steps of these techniques and what foods are best cooked using each method, you can cook just about anything. Throughout this book, you'll learn much more about the techniques, and soon you'll be able to start cooking without a recipe.

Dry-heat cooking and *moist-heat cooking* are the two main categories of cooking styles. Dry-heat cooking is most often used when you want to brown the food to develop a deep, rich flavor. Dry-heat cooking techniques include sautéing, frying, and grilling. Moist heat cooking is most often used to retain bright flavors and to tenderize what's being cooked; these techniques include boiling, simmering, poaching, steaming, and braising.

Dry-Heat Cooking Methods

Sautéing

The *sautéing* method uses high-heat cooking in a pan. Thin, tender cuts of meat such as chicken breasts and hamburgers are good for sautéing. This method is also used for heating vegetables and browning them a bit on the outside, which still leaves them firm on the inside. *Searing* and *stir-frying* are methods of sautéing.

The basic steps of sautéing are:

- Season the food being cooked.

- Put the food in a very hot pan lightly coated with oil.

- Cook on high heat until browning occurs.

- Turn the food and repeat the cooking process on the other side.

Grilling

Grilling is the process of cooking directly over a flame or other heat source. It's best to grill items that are less than $^1/_2$ inch (1.25cm) thick and tender, such as sliced summer squash, salmon, or beef steaks. The technique of *broiling* is a form of grilling but with the flame above the food rather than below.

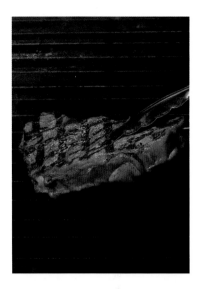

The basic steps of grilling are:

- Season and oil the food.
- Place the food on the hot grill and cook halfway.
- Turn the food and cook the rest of the way.

Frying

Frying uses hot oil to cook food. The process of deep-frying is often confused as a moist-heat cooking technique, but moist cooking uses water to penetrate the item being cooked in order to heat the food. Frying is a dry heat method because water doesn't exist in the oil. If the technique is used correctly, the oil doesn't penetrate into the food—it's only a conduit for the heat. This process is best used for delicate, quick-cooking items such as shrimp, onion rings, or chicken. In pan-frying, the oil only goes halfway up the sides of the food. In deep-frying the food is fully submerged in the oil.

The basic steps of pan-frying are:

- Season the food.
- Coat it with flour and bread crumbs.
- Place it in preheated oil and cook halfway.
- Turn the food and finish cooking.

Moist-Heat Cooking Methods

Boiling

The technique of *boiling* is cooking food submerged in a liquid that's 212°F (100°C). This process is often used with starches to hydrate and soften them. Examples are cooking potatoes for mashing and cooking pasta.

The basic steps of boiling are:

- Season the cooking liquid and bring it to a boil.
- Place the food to be cooked in the boiling liquid.

Simmering

Cooking food in a liquid at 180° to 210°F (82° to 99°C) is called *simmering*. Simmering is most often used for tough cuts of meat, or for delicate vegetables and starches. Examples of foods that are simmered are beef and vegetable soup, stocks, and corned beef.

The basic steps of simmering are:

- Heat the liquid to a boil.
- Season the food.
- Submerge the food in the liquid. Adjust the heat to keep within the 180° to 210°F (82° to 99°C) range.

Poaching

Poaching cooks food in a flavorful acidic liquid at 160° to 180°F (71° to 82°C). This technique can be used on tender, thin-cut foods. Cooking at this low temperature preserves more nutrients and the natural flavors of the food. This technique is often used for chicken or fish. *Shallow poaching* is a variation in which the liquid covers the food halfway and the pan is covered.

The basic steps of poaching are:

- Heat the liquid to a simmer.
- Season the food.
- Submerge the food in the liquid. Adjust the heat to keep in the 160° to 180°F (71° to 82°C) range.

Steaming

Steaming is cooking food in hot vapors, most often the steam from boiling water. Steaming is considered a nutritious method of cooking because fewer vitamins and minerals are leached out into the cooking medium compared with poaching or simmering. This method is most often used on vegetables, such as broccoli and asparagus.

The basic steps of steaming are:

- Heat liquid to the steaming point.
- Place the food in the steam above the liquid. Cover the pot to trap the steam in.
- After cooking through, vegetables should be chilled or served right away to retain nutrients.

Braising

Braising combines sautéing, steaming, and simmering. The best example of braising might be cooking a pot roast, where the meat is sautéed to brown on all sides and then put into a pot with liquid that comes one half to two thirds of the way up the sides of the meat. The liquid is brought up to a simmer and the pot is covered to hold in the steam. This technique is ideal for tough cuts of meat. *Stewing* is a form of braising in which the meat is cut into smaller pieces, sautéed, and completely submerged in the simmering liquid.

The basic steps of braising are:

- Season the food and cover it in oil.
- Add the food to a hot pan and brown on all sides.
- Add a flavorful liquid to the pan and bring up to 180° to 210°F (82° to 99°C)
- Maintain the temperature until the food is tender.

breakfast

In this chapter, you'll learn about the basic breakfast dishes and styles. This chapter starts off with eggs and moves on to pancakes, bacon, potatoes, and other breakfast staples. You'll even learn to make your own granola. Enjoy practicing and playing with variations of these recipes each morning.

Egg Basics

Eggs are high in protein, balanced in nutrition, low in cost, and readily available throughout most of the world. This makes them a popular food to start the day.

Following are a few things you should keep in mind when you buy and cook with eggs.

How to Buy Eggs

Eggs are graded by the USDA as they're packaged for sale. This grading system tells you the quality of the eggs at the time of packaging. Keep in mind these grades may change based on how long it takes the eggs to get to market, and at what temperature range they're kept.

Grade AA – These have a firm yolk and the white stands tall when broken onto a flat surface. The yolk is centered in the shell and the air pocket is very small.

Grade A – The yolk starts to flatten when cracked onto a flat surface. The white of the egg slowly spreads out. In the shell, the air pocket is a little larger than Grade AA.

Grade B – The yolk is loose and breaks easily. The white is watery when broken onto a flat surface. In the shell, the air pocket is large enough that the uncracked egg will float when placed in cold water.

Egg Sizes

Eggs are graded by size based on the weight of the egg without the shell.

Peewee	1.25 oz. (35.5g)
Small	1.5 oz. (42.5g)
Medium	1.75 oz. (49.5g)
Large	2 oz. (56.5g)
Extra Large	2.25 oz. (63.5g)
Jumbo	2.5 oz. (70.5g)

When purchasing eggs, there are a few things you need to keep in mind: size, grade, and freshness. And most importantly for flavor, how the chickens are raised.

The standard size of an egg is Large. This size is a 2-oz. (56.5g) egg, and the yolk and white are each nearly 1 oz. (28.5g). This is the standard by which recipes are written. For baking, in particular, you want to make sure you're buying only large eggs.

The USDA grades eggs based on the quality at packaging time. The date of grading is printed on the egg carton. When you purchase eggs, look for Grade AA eggs that are less than two weeks from inspection. The next best choice is Grade A eggs that are less than one week old.

Also look to see how the eggs are stored. Fresh eggs should be kept in a cooler that maintains a temperature of 32° to 39°F (0° to 3.9°C). For each day the egg is kept at room temperature, an equivalent of one week of aging of a cold egg occurs.

The biggest factor in the flavor of an egg is how the chicken is kept. For the highest-quality eggs, chickens should live in an outdoor coop that's moved regularly, which gives the chickens the opportunity to peck at the ground. By eating worms and insects, chickens produce eggs with higher levels of omega-3 fatty acids. These "good acids" produce orange color in the yolk and a much richer flavor, overall. The best place to find these eggs is your local farmers market.

Refrigerating Eggs

Eggs should be stored in a cold part of your refrigerator, but not on the door. The door tends to be the warmest area because warm air enters every time it's opened. Many appliance manufacturers put egg cradles in the doors, but this is not ideal. Eggs should be stored in the carton they're purchased in and on the top shelf of the refrigerator.

Safety Tips

There are a few food safety concerns you must consider when you use eggs. Check the date of inspection on the carton, and use the eggs within four to five weeks of the packaging date. Before using an egg, look for cracks and discard any cracked eggs immediately.

Because eggs contain so many nutrients, bacteria can grow quickly. You must treat eggs as a potentially hazardous food and wash your hands before and after handling them. Also, eggs should be cooked higher than 139°F (59.5°C). Consume cooked egg products within one hour, or chill below 35°F (1.6°C).

Brown Eggs or White?

Many people pay a premium for eggs with brown shells. The popular belief is that brown eggs have better flavor or are more nutritious. But the color of the shell is determined by the breed of the chicken, and doesn't affect the nutritional quality of the egg.

4

 1 minute

 12 minutes

INGREDIENTS

4 eggs
Enough water to cover
 eggs

TOOLS

4 qt. (4L) stainless steel
 pot
1 qt. (1L) kitchen bowl

Boiled Eggs

Boiled eggs are actually not boiled, but simmered. If the water was at a true boil, the eggs would float about bumping into each other and breaking open.

 Don't use aluminum pots and pans when working with eggs. A chemical reaction occurs naturally with aluminum and turns the egg yolks a brown or green color. Stainless steel or cast iron pots and pans work best for eggs.

1 Put water in the pot and bring to a boil. While the water is heating, put the eggs in a bowl of warm tap water to bring them up to room temperature. If the eggs float, they're too old to use. Fresh eggs will sink to the bottom of the bowl.

2 After the water comes to a boil, remove eggs from the bowl and place in the pot. Immediately turn down the heat to simmer. You want the water to have a bubble coming to the surface every 3 to 5 seconds. Cook 4 minutes for a creamy center. For fully boiled eggs, cook 10 minutes.

3 Drain the water and run cold water into the pot. This will help pull the shells away from the whites, making them easier to peel. Serve immediately or put into the refrigerator to cool.

BREAKFAST

Fried Eggs

Too often when you ask for a fried egg you get something that has completely browned around the edges. A fried egg should not look like your grandma's old doily.

 2

 1 minute

 3 minutes

INGREDIENTS

4 large eggs

2 TB. whole butter

¼ tsp. sea salt

Pinch black pepper

TOOLS

8-inch (20cm) stainless steel sauté pan

High-temp rubber spatula

1 Place the sauté pan on medium flame to preheat. Melt butter in the sauté pan. The pan should be hot enough to melt the butter but not allow it to start to brown.

2 Crack the eggs into the pan of melted butter. Let them set for a minute, then spoon the butter from around the eggs onto the top of the yolk. Continue to do this for about 1 minute until the white starts to form on top of the yolk.

3 When the eggs have cooked to the point where they're glistening but not cooked through, flip them over with the spatula. Let them set for 1 minute for over easy eggs, 2 minutes for over medium, or 3 minutes for over hard. Remove from the heat and place onto serving plates.

The eggs will continue to cook for several minutes after you remove them from the heat.

 Eggs can be fried as over easy, over medium, or over hard.

2

 1 minute

 3 minutes

INGREDIENTS

4 large eggs

1 TB. water

2 TB. whole butter

¼ tsp. sea salt

Pinch black pepper

TOOLS

8-inch (20cm) stainless
 steel sauté pan

Mixing bowl

Whisk

High-temp rubber spatula

Scrambled Eggs

The secret to fluffy, flavorful eggs is low heat and lots of butter. Well-prepared scrambled eggs should be golden yellow without any browning.

1 Place the sauté pan on low flame to preheat. Crack the eggs into the mixing bowl and add water, salt, and pepper. Whisk gently to break the yolks, but not so much that the whites and yolks are fully integrated.

2 Melt butter in the sauté pan. The pan should be hot enough to melt the butter but not allow it to start to brown. Pour eggs into the pan with the melted butter. Let eggs sit for a minute, then turn in from the outside to the middle with the spatula.

3 When the eggs have cooked to the point where they're glistening but not cooked through, remove from heat. Divide onto serving plates. The eggs will continue to cook for several minutes after you remove them from the heat.

How to Crack an Egg

The first thing to know is that tapping the egg on a flat surface will help to develop a uniform crack around the middle. Once the shell is cracked, pull the two sides apart so the egg falls through the middle. Another secret of chefs: stainless steel will naturally attract the shells like a magnet. So if you're cracking your eggs into a stainless steel bowl, you don't need to worry about fishing out stray shell pieces.

Variations

Want to bring the basic scrambled eggs up a notch? Try these variations to give your breakfast a kick.

Herbs: Always use fresh herbs with eggs. Dried herbs won't have time to soften in the eggs. Chives, Italian parsley, chervil, and tarragon are classically paired with eggs. Fold in 2 teaspoons of the chopped herb at the end of the cooking process for each recipe.

Curry: Add ½ teaspoon of curry powder to the eggs before whisking.

Ham: Add ½ cup of chopped ham to the butter before adding the eggs to the sauté pan.

Cheese: Add 2 tablespoons of your favorite shredded cheese to the eggs when they're added to the pan.

Smoked salmon: Add 2 slices of smoked salmon to the butter before adding the eggs to the pan.

Onions: Add 2 tablespoons of small diced onions to the butter before adding the eggs to the pan.

Crab: Add 4 tablespoons of crab meat to the butter before adding the eggs to the pan.

BREAKFAST

Poached Eggs

If you have fresh eggs, it's pretty easy to make a great-looking poached egg. The important thing to remember is that the liquid should not be boiling when the eggs are added. If it's boiling, the water will toss the egg around and break it.

 2

 1 minute

 3 minutes

INGREDIENTS

4 large eggs
Water to cover eggs
½ tsp. lemon juice
¼ tsp. sea salt
Pinch black pepper

TOOLS

12-inch (30.5cm) stain-
 less steel pot
Mixing bowl
Slotted kitchen spoon

1   Place the pot over low flame to pre-heat with water and lemon juice. Crack eggs into the mixing bowl. When the water comes to a boil, remove from heat. From the bowl, drop each egg into the hot water individually.

2   Return the pan to the burner. The water should show a bubble about every 5 seconds but shouldn't boil. If it bubbles more than desired, turn off the flame. Allow to cook for 2 minutes.

3   Remove eggs from the water with a slotted spoon, allowing the excess water to drip away. Place eggs on serving plate, and season with salt and pepper.

1

 1 minute

 3 minutes

INGREDIENTS

3 large eggs

1 TB. milk

2 TB. whole butter

¼ tsp. sea salt

Pinch black pepper

TOOLS

8-inch (20cm) stainless
 steel sauté pan

Mixing bowl

Whisk

High-temperature rubber
 spatula

Omelet

Omelets can be served for any meal. There are variations from France that are folded once, from Italy that are folded twice, and from Spain that are never folded. This simple recipe is similar to a French omelet.

1 Preheat the sauté pan over medium flame. Crack eggs into the mixing bowl, and add milk, salt, and pepper. Whisk gently to break the yolks, but not so much that whites and yolks are fully integrated.

2 Melt the butter in the sauté pan. The pan should be hot enough to melt the butter but not allow it to brown. Pour eggs into the pan with the melted butter. Using the spatula, lift the outer edges of the eggs, allowing uncooked egg to run underneath.

3 When the eggs are mostly cooked, to the point where they're lightly glistening, remove from the heat. Add cheese and pre-heated filling ingredients to ½ of the eggs.

4 Slowly slide the omelet out of the pan and onto the plate. When it's ¾ of the way onto the plate, pull the pan across the top of the plate so the omelet folds over on itself.

BREAKFAST

Separating the yolk using a plastic water bottle

There are many ways to separate the yolk from the white of an egg. The cleanest and most effective way is to use an empty water bottle. To do this, crack the egg into a bowl. Squeeze the empty water bottle and place the opening of the bottle over the egg yolk so it's touching the yolk. Release your squeeze on the bottle so it sucks the yolk into the bottle and leaves the white behind. Hold the opening of the bottle over an empty bowl. Squeeze the bottle and the yolk will come out.

Variations

Except for cheese, the fillings for the omelet should be heated in a separate pan and added while they're still hot. Add cheese at room temperature, just before adding the other hot fillings.

Cheese: Add ¼ cup shredded cheddar.

Denver: Cook 2 tablespoons small diced ham, 1 tablespoon small diced onions, and 1 tablespoon small diced green pepper over medium heat for 3 minutes with 1 tablespoon olive oil. Add 2 tablespoons shredded cheddar cheese to the omelet before adding the heated ham mixture.

Spinach and mushrooms: Cook ½ cup chopped mushrooms over high heat for 5 minutes with 1 tablespoon olive oil. Add 1 tablespoon small diced onions, one clove minced garlic, and 1 packed cup baby spinach. Cook the mixture for 4 more minutes over medium heat.

Crab and chives: Cook 1 tablespoon small diced onions over medium heat for 3 minutes with 1 tablespoon olive oil. Add 2 tablespoons lump crab meat. Add 1 tablespoon sour cream and 1 teaspoon chopped chives to the omelet before adding the heated mixture.

4

 10 minutes

 48 minutes

INGREDIENTS

½ lb. (225g) all-purpose flour

1 TB. granulated sugar

½ TB. baking soda

1 tsp. baking powder

1 tsp. kosher salt

1½ cups buttermilk

2 oz. (60mL) unsalted butter, melted

2 large eggs, whisked

Pan spray

TOOLS

Sifter

2 mixing bowls

Rubber spatula

8-inch (20cm) sauté pan

4 oz. (120mL) ladle

Offset spatula

Pancakes

In this easy pancake recipe, the wet and dry ingredients are measured separately and mixed just before they're used. The mixing has to be done quickly, and there may still be little lumps left—a common trait of quick breads.

1 Sift together flour, sugar, baking powder, baking soda, and salt in one bowl large enough to hold all ingredients (fig. a).

2 In a second bowl, mix together the buttermilk, melted butter, and whisked eggs (fig. b).

3 Preheat the pan over medium flame. In the first bowl, form a little well in the middle of the dry ingredients and pour in the liquid ingredients (fig. c).

4 Using a rubber spatula, swirl the liquid moving from inside the well into the dry ingredients (fig. d). Incorporate the wet and dry ingredients using this mixing method so there are still little lumps of dry ingredients, but nothing bigger than a pea.

5 Spray the hot pan with pan spray and ladle in 4 ounces (120mL) of batter (fig. e). In 3 to 4 minutes, the batter should start to set up and bubbles should appear at the top of the batter.

6 When the top of the pancake is covered with bubbles, use the offset spatula to turn the pancake (fig. f). Cook for another minute on this side. Remove from the pan onto a serving plate.

 Chef's Tip

Don't be alarmed if the first pancake doesn't look the best; the subsequent pancakes will look better. Repeat the process until the batter has been used. You should have about 12 pancakes when finished.

BREAKFAST

French Toast

French toast was created to use up leftover bread baked the previous day. Today's breads stay fresh much longer, so there's less concern about wasting. But French toast has remained a popular breakfast dish that can be made with many types of breads.

 4

 10 minutes

 30 minutes

INGREDIENTS

4 oz. (120mL) heavy cream

½ tsp. ground cinnamon

¼ tsp. vanilla extract

¼ tsp. kosher salt

10 large eggs, whisked

8 slices bread of choice

8 TB. unsalted butter

TOOLS

Mixing bowl

Whisk

Sheet pan

Tongs

12-inch (30.5cm) heavy-bottomed stainless steel sauté pan

Offset spatula

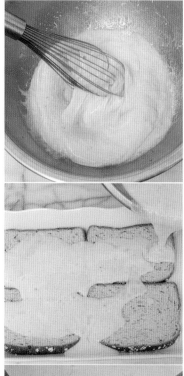

1 Lightly whisk together heavy cream and cinnamon just to combine. Add vanilla, salt, and eggs and lightly whisk.

2 Lay the bread out on a sheet pan. Pour batter over the bread evenly. Allow to set for 3 to 4 minutes so batter is soaked into the bread.

3 Place a pan over a medium flame and melt 2 tablespoons of butter. Add 2 slices soaked bread to the pan. Allow the French toast to cook for 3 minutes, turn, and cook for 2 minutes on the other side.

4 Move to a serving plate and finish with the topping(s) of your choice. Common toppings include powdered sugar, whipped cream, maple syrup, and/or fruit compote.

 Chef's Note

Most spices come from seeds, roots, and barks. This means they don't dissolve very well in water, but they do dissolve in fats or oils. In this recipe, the cinnamon is added with the heavy cream so the fats in the cream help dissolve the cinnamon. If you were to use milk instead of heavy cream, the cinnamon would just float to the top of the mixture and end up covering only the first piece of French toast you make.

8

 10 minutes

2½ hours

INGREDIENTS

½ cup brown sugar

3 oz. (90mL) hot tap water

2 oz. (60mL) peanut oil

1½ cups old-fashioned rolled oats

½ cup wheat germ

1 tsp. sea salt

2 TB. whole wheat flour

1 TB. corn starch

1 TB. corn meal

½ cup chopped pecans

TOOLS

Small mixing bowl

Large mixing bowl

Sheet pan

Offset spatula

Airtight container

Granola (or Muesli)

Grains are one of the most widely consumed breakfast foods in the world. They're eaten in many forms, from steaming hot cereals to cold cereals and granolas. This granola recipe makes a great healthy breakfast and can be consumed with milk, yogurt, or nut milks.

1 In the small mixing bowl, combine brown sugar, water, and oil. In the larger mixing bowl, combine all the dry ingredients and mix to evenly distribute all ingredients.

2 Mix the brown sugar liquid with the dry ingredients. This should be just moist, not completely wet. Spread the mixture on the sheet pan.

3 Place in a 200°F (94°C) oven until dry. This will take about 2 hours. Turn the granola in the pan every 30 minutes using the offset spatula.

When the granola is dry, allow it to cool. Place in an airtight container until needed.

When serving the granola, combine or layer with dried fruits, nuts, and yogurt or milk.

Bacon

Pork is a traditional breakfast favorite, usually in a cured form such as bacon, ham, or sausage. If you cook these meats on the stovetop, they spatter oils on surrounding surfaces. The best way to avoid this is to roast them in the oven.

 8

 5 minutes

 12 hours

INGREDIENTS

1 lb. (450g) sliced bacon

TOOLS

18 x 13 sheet pan

Tongs

Hot pad

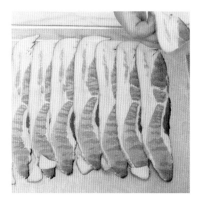

1 Preheat the oven to 400°F (204°C). Remove bacon from the package and line up in a single layer on the sheet pan. The slices can be placed right next to one another—touching is encouraged.

2 Place the bacon in the oven. Roast for 12 minutes, and check for doneness. Thicker-sliced bacon will take longer to cook. When it reaches your desired doneness, remove the pan from the oven.

3 Immediately remove bacon from the sheet pan and place it on a serving plate lined with paper towels. This will allow excess fat to drain from the bacon.

 Chef's Note

Bacon is a favorite food around the world, but not all bacon is created equal. All bacon is salt cured and then smoked. But in different countries, various cuts of meat are used to make the bacon. In Great Britain, bacon comes from the shoulder of the pig. In Canada, the loin of the pig is used. And bacon in the United States comes from the belly of the pig.

4

 10 minutes

 20 minutes

INGREDIENTS

4 russet potatoes

2 TB. peanut oil

1 TB. kosher salt

1 tsp. coarse ground pepper

2 TB. whole butter

TOOLS

Potato peeler

Mixing bowl

Heavy-bottomed 12-inch (30.5cm) sauté pan

Offset spatula

Breakfast Potatoes

Potatoes are a staple in homes and breakfast restaurants around the world. For many people, the overnight fast leaves the body low on sugars. The starch in potatoes changes to consumable sugar quickly, giving the body a much needed wake-up call.

1 Peel and rinse the potatoes (fig. a), and cut into the desired diced, sliced, or shredded shape (fig. b). As you cut them, put the pieces into a bowl and cover with water. Potatoes will turn grey or brown if left exposed to air when they're raw.

2 Place the sauté pan over medium heat. Drain the water from potatoes. Place the oil in the pan, and add the potatoes (fig. c). Salt and pepper to taste. Cover the pan and don't check for 10 minutes (fig. d). The steam will help cook the potatoes.

3 Remove the lid and turn the potatoes with a spatula (fig. e). If they're sticking, leave the lid off and cook a little longer. When they turn brown on the bottom, they'll stop sticking.

4 Allow them to cook an additional 5 minutes uncovered and without turning again. Add the whole butter and allow it to melt into the potatoes (fig. f).

5 Taste to make sure the seasoning is right and the potatoes are cooked through. When seasoning is adjusted and potatoes are cooked, remove to a serving plate.

 Chef's Note

People often confuse the names of breakfast potatoes. They're primarily named by the way the potatoes are cut.

If the potatoes are *shredded*, they're referred to as *hash browns* or *hashed browns*.

If the potatoes are *medium diced*, they're called *cottage fries*.

If the potatoes are *sliced* (with skin on or off) they're called *home fries*.

sauces and condiments

In this chapter, you'll learn the main types of sauces. We start with contemporary salsas and emulsions, and then teach you the five classic mother sauces. Good sauces can elevate your creations from good to fabulous, and learning the fundamentals of making the sauces that follow will help you wow your dinner guests with many exciting dishes.

Sauces and Condiments

Sauces are often an afterthought to the foods we create. But a well-made sauce can make a meal an experience people will remember. If you go to a restaurant and have a good steak, you might walk away thinking, *That was a pretty good steak.* But if you have a steak served with a mushroom demi-glace, you walk away thinking, *Wow, that steak was amazing!* Sauces are an easy way to elevate your meal from pretty good to amazing.

Sauces are used to season, flavor, and enhance other foods. They fall into a few categories: mother sauces, small sauces, salsas and chutneys, and contemporary sauces. Mother sauces are defined as sauces that can be made in large batches and kept to make smaller amounts of other, more specific sauces. Classical French cooking says there are five mother sauces:

Hollandaise: butter and egg yolk emulsion

Béchamel: basic cream sauce

Velouté: basic chicken sauce

Espagnole: basic beef sauce

Tomato: tomato-based sauce

Salsas and chutneys are fresh fruits and/or vegetables mixed together with flavorful ingredients. Salsas are never cooked and are served cold; chutneys are cooked and then chilled and served cold. Neither salsas nor chutneys contain outside thickeners.

Then there's the contemporary sauce category. In this group are sauces that often look like they contain a mother sauce, but do not. These are often used in regional or traditional dishes.

When making a sauce for a dish, you have to think of the plate as a whole. The sauce is a bridge that connects all the different flavors, and it should fill in any gaps of missing flavors on the tongue. Most of all, it should taste good on its own but never overpower the flavors of the other foods on the plate.

The Physiology of Taste

The taste buds play an essential part in how we perceive food.

There are five main tastes: **sweet, salt, acid, bitter,** and **umami** (savory). They concentrate in clusters on your tongue, much as like-minded people in a neighborhood. Most of the sweet taste buds live on the tip of your tongue. On the front side are the salt taste buds, and further back on the sides are the acid taste buds. In the very back are the bitter taste buds. And through the middle, enhancing and connecting with the other four, is the umami superhighway. In a neighborhood in any city, there are always a few people who just don't seem to fit, and the same is true with taste buds—sometimes you'll have a sweet taste bud hanging out in the acid area of the tongue.

As a cook, think about tasting food with more of a flat tongue instead of curled. Make sure the food touches all parts of the tongue so you can really understand the complex flavor balance. Food manufacturers understand that the body craves a combination of these five flavors. Soda manufacturers have even gone to the next level, and analyzed the ways people in different geographic areas drink. They've discovered that in some parts of the world it's more common to drink out of a bottle, allowing a liquid to hit the middle of the tongue and slide down the throat. They'll often increase the amount of sugar and acid in a liquid so they will more likely be felt on the tongue.

Understanding how the taste of your food is perceived will help you develop memorable dishes.

SAUCES AND CONDIMENTS

Pico de Gallo (Salsa)

Salsa, with its bright, fresh flavors, is the most widely consumed condiment in the world. It brings out all five tastes and adds hot capsaicin to the mouth feel. This recipe can be used with tortilla chips, or even as a flavor enhancer for meats and vegetables.

 4

 15 minutes

 none

INGREDIENTS

2 beefsteak-size tomatoes

2 green onions, diced

1 clove garlic, minced

5 stems and leaves fresh cilantro, chopped

1 jalapeño, seeded and small diced

1 oz. (30mL) lemon juice

1 TB. sea salt

TOOLS

Serving bowl

French knife

Cutting board

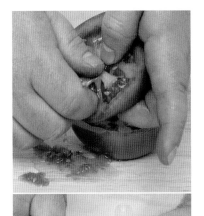

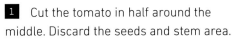

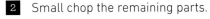

1 Cut the tomato in half around the middle. Discard the seeds and stem area.

2 Small chop the remaining parts.

3 Combine all remaining ingredients. Taste the flavor, and add more salt, lemon juice, or jalapeño as desired.

Store leftover salsa in an airtight container in the refrigerator for up to a week.

 Chef's Tip

Most of us can relate to purchasing tomatoes that are white and mealy on the inside and don't have real tomato flavor which is a result of the tomatoes being picked before they're ripe. You should always take into consideration the quality of ingredients you use when you're preparing foods, and this is particularly important in this salsa recipe. If you can't pick or find fresh tomatoes that were grown to full maturity, the flavors won't be the same. You'll end up with a better sauce if you use canned diced tomatoes instead of fruit that isn't mature. Also, tomatoes that have been refrigerated at the grocery store will lack the rich flavors of freshly picked fruit, so don't store your tomatoes in the refrigerator at home.

4

 10 minutes

 none

INGREDIENTS

¾ cup ketchup

¼ cup prepared horse-radish (often found in the produce section of the grocery store)

2 tsp. lime juice

¼ tsp. hot pepper sauce

TOOLS

Whisk

Serving bowl

Cocktail Sauce

Classic cocktail sauce is most associated with hors d'oeuvres, such as shrimp. Don't assume that this quick and easy recipe results in a bland, unexciting sauce; hot pepper and horseradish make this a rich, spicy sauce with a very delicate balance of flavors.

1 Combine all the ingredients in the serving bowl.

2 Whisk the ingredients together.

Taste the sauce with the food you'll be serving with it. You want to make sure the flavor of the sauce doesn't overpower the taste of the main ingredient. If it does, dilute it a little with tomato sauce or tomato paste.

 Chef's Tip
You can use fresh horseradish root in this recipe, if it's available. If you do, be sure to shred the root 24 hours before you need it—the flavors intensify after it's shredded. For this recipe, shred ¼ cup horserad-ish root and allow it to sit overnight. By substituting the fresh root for the prepared horseradish, you'll get a sauce with a more refined and intense flavor and a firmer, finished texture.

SAUCES AND CONDIMENTS

Guacamole

More people are discovering and enjoying nutritious avocados. They're rich in good fats, and seasonings give them an appealing mouth feel. This recipe teaches you how easy it is to remove the avocado seed and make delicious guacamole.

 4

 10 minutes

INGREDIENTS

2 ripe avocados (slightly soft)

2 oz. (60mL) lime juice

1 green onion, chopped

5 stems and leaves of cilantro, chopped

2 TB. tomato, seeded and small diced

1 clove garlic, minced

½ tsp. Mexican oregano

1 jalapeño, seeded and small diced

1 tsp. sea salt

¼ tsp. black pepper

TOOLS

Mixing bowl

Wooden spoon

Serving bowl

Chef's knife

Cutting board

1 Place the avocado on a cutting board and push a sharp knife along a line from stem to bloom end. The knife will stop when it gets to the seed (fig. a). Leave the knife against the seed and turn the avocado until the knife meets the starting cut. Remove the knife.

2 Holding a cut half in each hand, twist in opposite directions and pull apart (fig. b).

3 Put the half with the seed on the cutting board, seed facing up. Thump the top of the seed with the sharp knife edge so it penetrates about ¼ inch (6.35mm). Twist the seed with the knife until it pops out (fig c.).

4 Run a tablespoon between the skin and the flesh of the avocado. Place the flesh in a mixing bowl. Sprinkle generously with lime juice to get juice on every part (fig. d).

5 Mash the avocado against the sides of the bowl with a wooden spoon until you have just a few lumps (fig. e).

6 Add remaining ingredients and mix (fig. f). Taste the guacamole with whatever you're serving. Adjust flavorings as desired and transfer to the serving bowl.

If you're not serving immediately, put the seed in with the guacamole to keep it fresh, cover, and refrigerate.

 Chef's Tip

Avocado flesh will oxidize and turn brown quickly when exposed to air. The best way to prevent this is to mix in the citrus juice right away. If you're going to store the avocado for more than an hour, put the seed in with it.

1 pint

 6 minutes

 none

INGREDIENTS

2 large eggs

1 tsp. dry mustard powder

1 TB. white vinegar

1 oz. (30mL) lemon juice

12 oz. (355mL) vegetable oil

¼ tsp. white pepper

½ tsp. celery salt

TOOLS

Tall plastic cup or glass

Immersion blender

Mayonnaise

Mayonnaise is readily available in stores, but you don't have the flexibility to create unique flavors if you use pre-made products. You can substitute any vinegar for white in this recipe, such as raspberry for a raspberry mayonnaise that's used in a lobster salad recipe.

1 Measure all ingredients and hold them at room temperature for 15 minutes before you use them (really cold ingredients can cause the mayonnaise to not come together). Once the ingredients have been warmed, break the eggs into the tall cup and add the mustard powder, vinegar, and lemon juice (fig. a).

2 Begin blending the ingredients immediately (fig. b). Vinegar and lemon juice, both acids, will sour the egg and once you add the acids you must purée the mixture right away.

3 As soon as the initial mixture is combined, add the oil while the blender is running (fig. c). Pour it in one steady stream, lifting the blender in and out of the liquid. It shouldn't take more than 1 minute to add all the oil.

4 Add the seasonings and use the immersion blender to combine them. Taste and adjust consistency and flavor as needed.

 Chef's Tip

If the mayonnaise is too runny, add more oil while the blender is running until it reaches the thickness you desire. If the mayonnaise is too thick, add a little more lemon juice or water. If it tastes too acidic, add sugar to balance the flavor.

a

b

c

Variations

Remoulade (tartar sauce): Add 2 tablespoons of chopped dill pickle, 2 tablespoons of capers (rinsed), 1 tablespoon of chopped chives, and one clove of minced garlic.

Aioli (garlic): Add 4 cloves of garlic, minced.

Avocado: Use lime juice instead of lemon. Add the flesh of one avocado and purée into mayonnaise with an emersion blender.

Curry: Use lime juice instead of lemon. Add 1 tablespoon curry powder and 1 clove of garlic, minced. Purée together.

Chipotle: Use lime instead of lemon. Add one chile pepper from a can of chipotle packed in adobo sauce. Purée together.

Cilantro lime: Use lime instead of lemon. Add 20 cilantro leaves and 1 clove of garlic, minced. Puree together.

Pesto: Purée in ¼ cup of pesto.

SAUCES AND CONDIMENTS

Hollandaise Sauce

Hollandaise is a semi-permanent emulsion, and egg yolks keep the liquids suspended in the clarified butter. Be careful to keep the temperature of all the ingredients between 110°F and 144°F (43°C and 62°C). If cooler, the butter will solidify; if warmer, the eggs will start to cook.

 4

 10 minutes

 2 minutes

1 Heat 1 cup of water in the pot to a simmer and turn the heat down to low. Meanwhile, combine peppercorns, vinegar, and 1 ounce (30mL) of water in a small sauté pan and place on high heat. Allow the liquid to boil down until it reduces by half (fig. a). Remove and reserve.

2 Place the egg yolks in a metal bowl and strain the vinegar-pepper liquid into it (fig. b). Place the bowl over the simmering pot of water. Whisk the yolks, aerating and cooking them (fig. c). After about 1 minute, you should be able to draw a line through the middle of the yolks without them immediately coming back together (fig. d). At this point, remove the bowl from the simmering pot.

3 After removing the bowl from the cooktop, slowly dribble 1 ounce (30mL) of clarified butter into the yolks while vigorously whisking. Once the butter has emulsified, add the lemon juice.

4 Add the rest of the butter in one steady stream while whisking. You should be drawing the whisk across the bottom of the bowl and up around the top of the liquid. Using this motion, you'll incorporate air into the Hollandaise, making it lighter and softer on the palate.

5 Add salt and cayenne pepper. Taste and adjust the flavors and thickness. If too thin, whisk in more clarified butter. If too thick, add a touch of warm water.

6 Pour the finished Hollandaise into a coffee carafe to hold at the right temperature. It's being held at a temperature that allows bacteria to grow, so it's important to keep the sauce for only a couple of hours before discarding.

INGREDIENTS

1 cup water

5 white peppercorns

1 oz. (30mL) white vinegar

1 oz. (30mL) water

2 large egg yolks

1 TB. lemon juice

¾ cup clarified butter, melted but not hot

1 tsp. sea salt

¼ tsp. cayenne pepper

TOOLS

2 qt. (2L) pot

Small sauté pan

Metal mixing bowl

Whisk

Wire strainer

Coffee carafe

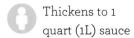 Thickens to 1
quart (1L) sauce

 2 minutes

 2–120 minutes

INGREDIENTS

2 oz. (60mL) clarified
 butter

½ cup cake flour

TOOLS

Sauté pan
Whisk

Roux

Roux is a combination of fat and flour that's used to thicken classic sauces and gravies. The ratio of 2 ounces (55g) (by weight) of roux is enough to thicken 1 pint (470mL) of liquid when the roux is a blond color.

1 Put the butter in the sauté pan and melt over medium heat. After the butter has melted, whisk in the flour a little at a time, fully incorporating the flour into the butter each time.

2 Cook over medium heat until the desired color is achieved. Remove from heat. Pour into a separate container to stop the cooking process.

Why Cake Flour?

Flours are classified by how much starch and protein (gluten) they contain. In this case, we want higher amounts of starch to thicken. Glutens also tend to make sauces murkier in color, so we want less protein. Cake flour is high starch, low protein, so it's the ideal choice for making a roux. All purpose (AP) flour is moderate starch, moderate protein. Bread flour is moderate starch, high protein.

Types of Roux

The longer the roux is cooked before adding any liquid, the more color and flavor that will develop. This longer cooking also means the starches in the flour start to break down and won't thicken a liquid as much.

White roux ———
used for Béchamel

Blond roux ———
used for Velouté

Brown roux ———
Used for Brown Sauce

Brick roux ———
Used for Cajun and Creole recipes

Variations

Cream gravy: Season with salt and black pepper.

Sausage gravy: Sauté 1 pound (450g) sausage, add 2 tablespoons flour to a hot pan, and mix with cooked sausage. Mix Béchamel into the sausage and flour.

Cheese sauce: Used for homemade macaroni and cheese. Heat Béchamel and add 8 ounces (240mL) of grated cheese of your choice. Finish with a dash of Worcestershire sauce and 1 teaspoon of dry mustard.

Mornay: Traditional with fish and seafood. Add 4 ounces (120mL) of grated Swiss cheese, 1 ounce of Parmesan, and finish with 2 tablespoons of whole butter.

Basic White Gravy (Béchamel)

Béchamel sauce is named for Louis de Béchamel, steward to Louis XIV of France. It's a rich sauce, and one of the easiest to make. Many restaurants make gallons of this each week to use in their different cream soups and sauces.

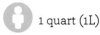 1 quart (1L)

 10 minutes

 1 hour

INGREDIENTS

¼ cup onion, chopped
1 oz. (30mL) vegetable oil
4 oz. (120mL) white roux
1½ qt. (1.5L) milk

TOOLS

2-qt. (2L) sauce pot
High-temp rubber spatula
Whisk
Strainer
Bowl

1 Set the pot over medium heat and add the oil and onions (fig. a). Cook until they're translucent, but have not developed any brown color.

2 Add the roux to the pot (fig. b). Heat and spread it around the pot. When it starts to bubble, you're ready to add the dairy.

3 Slowly pour the milk into the pot while vigorously whisking (fig. c). When all the roux is incorporated into the milk, let the sauce simmer for 1 hour on low.

4 As foam develops on top of the sauce, use a ladle to skim across the top and capture the foam. Discard these skimmings.

5 After 1 hour, strain the sauce through a mesh screen strainer or a double layer of cheesecloth (fig. d). Store this basic sauce until it's needed for finishing.

 Essential Technique: Simmering

Simmering is a low-temperature, moist-heat cooking technique where the liquid is kept at a temperature between 180°F and 210°F (82°C and 99°C) and below the boiling point of 212°F (100°C) when the moist qualities disappear. In this recipe, we simmer the sauce so the glutens in the flour used in the roux separate from the flour and float to the top of the sauce where you can skim them off. If the proteins are left in the sauce, it will become cloudy and have a pastelike flavor.

 1 quart (1L)

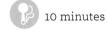 10 minutes

 1 hour

INGREDIENTS

1½ qt. (1.5L) white stock
(chicken, fish, or veal)
4 oz. (120mL) blond roux

TOOLS

2-qt. (2L) pot
Whisk
Strainer
Bowl

Basic Chicken Sauce (Velouté)

Velouté is the most often used of the mother sauces. It's a white stock made from veal, chicken, or fish and thickened with roux. This blank canvas can be painted to carry the end flavors of small sauce variations, and is used mainly for making soups.

1 Put the blond roux in the pot and heat until it begins to bubble (fig. a). Whisk in the cold white stock (fig. b). Bring to a boil, then reduce the heat to low. Simmer for 1 hour.

2 As foam or scum develops on the top of the sauce, use a ladle to skim across the top and capture the foam (fig. c). Discard these skimmings.

3 After 1 hour, strain the sauce through a mesh screen strainer or a double layer of cheesecloth (fig. d).

Store this basic sauce until needed for finishing.

 Essential Technique: Skimming

Skimming is important when making stocks, soups, and sauces. As these liquids simmer, the glutens, oils, and bloods float to the top. If you pull the simmering pot one fourth of the way off the burner, the liquid will heat up across one side, causing it to rise and cool across the top, and then sink back down the other side of the pot. This convection flow will make skimming easier. As the folates go across the top, they'll accumulate on the cooler side of the pot. You can put the ladle in the liquid so the only thing that can flow into the bowl of the ladle is the debris to be removed.

a

b

c

d

Variations

Soups: When making soups, sweat the main flavoring ingredient, add velouté, and simmer. To make a cream soup, finish this with Béchamel.

Sauce Vin Blanc: White wine sauce. Add 4 ounces (120mL) of white wine and 4 ounces (120mL) of heavy cream to the velouté. Simmer until it has reduced by half.

Sauce Aurora: Add 1 tablespoon of tomato paste to the velouté. Simmer until the sauce is reduced by half.

Normandy: This sauce is often used with fish. Add 4 ounces (110g) of mushrooms and allow to simmer until it has reduced by half. Finish by whisking in 1 egg yolk.

Variations

Robert: Add ½ cup diced onions, and 1 tablespoon butter. Heat the onions until translucent. Add ½ cup white wine. Add 1 quart brown sauce to the pot over medium flame and reduce sauce by half. Finish with ¼ teaspoon dry mustard powder and a pinch of sugar.

Mushroom: Put ½ cup sliced mushrooms and 2 tablespoons butter in a 2-quart (2L) pot on medium heat. Cook mushrooms for 20 minutes. Add 1 quart (1L) brown sauce and reduce sauce by half.

Red wine demi-glace: Add ½ cup diced onions and 1 tablespoon butter. Heat the onions until translucent. Add ½ cup red wine. Add 1 quart brown sauce to the pot over medium flame and reduce sauce by half.

Basic Brown Gravy (Espagnole)

 1 quart (1L)

 20 minutes

 2 hours

Brown sauce is a versatile mother sauce that's often used with beef. It's full bodied and very rich when finished. The main small sauce made from this is demiglace. This is a straight reduction of the brown sauce.

INGREDIENTS

2 oz. (60mL) vegetable oil

1 cup onions, chopped

½ cup carrots, chopped

½ cup celery, chopped

2 TB. tomato paste

1½ qt. (1.5L) brown stock

4 oz. (120mL) brown roux

1 sachet d'épices:

    1 bay leaf

    2 stems of parsley

    1 clove of garlic, crushed

    5 whole black peppercorns

    1 tsp. thyme leaves

1   Combine oil, onions, and carrots in the pot and place on medium heat (fig. a). Allow to cook, stirring every 4 to 5 minutes. You know when you're ready to go on to the next step when the onions are completely brown and the carrots are starting to brown.

2   Add the celery and tomato paste to the pot (fig. b). Continue to cook on medium heat until the paste changes from a red to an orange color. You need to keep slowly stirring and scraping the bottom of the pot. If you don't, the sugars in the tomato paste will burn.

3   Add the stock and bring it to a simmer. Vigorously whisk in the cold roux. It should be lump free when fully mixed. Simmer 1 hour, skimming the fats and solids that float to the top every 15 minutes. After 1 hour, add the sachet (fig. c).

4   After 15 additional simmering minutes, strain through a fine mesh strainer (fig. d). Keep the liquid brown sauce and discard the solids.

TOOLS

Cutting board

2-qt. (2L) sauce pot

Whisk

Fine mesh strainer

Bowl

 Chef's Tip

Mirepoix is the term used for 50 percent onions, 25 percent carrots, and 25 percent celery. This is a common base of flavors in France and the United States. In many parts of Asia it's ginger, garlic, and scallion (GGS). In Cajun foods it's onions, celery, and green bell peppers.

 1 quart (1L)

 10 minutes

 20 minutes

INGREDIENTS

2 oz. (60mL) olive oil

¼ cup small diced onions

1 TB minced garlic

1 qt. (1L) canned diced
  tomatoes packed in
  tomato puree

5 leaves basil, cut into a
  chiffonade

Sea salt and black pepper
  to taste

TOOLS

2-qt. (2L) pot

High-temp rubber spatula

Immersion blender

Classic Tomato Sauce

Classically, tomato sauce was made with pork bones and veal stock and simmered for hours because people long believed that straight tomatoes could be poisonous. The Bolognese variation that follows is more like that old classic tomato sauce recipe.

1 Put the pot on the stove over medium heat and add oil and onions (fig. a). Cook until they're translucent, but have not developed any brown color.

2 Add the garlic. As soon as you can smell the garlic cooking (2 minutes), add the tomatoes (fig. b). Continue to cook over medium heat.

3 When the tomatoes start to boil, remove the pot from the stove. Purée the mixture in the pot using an immersion blender (fig. c).

4 Finish the sauce by mixing in the basil (fig. d). Season with salt and pepper as desired. If the sauce is going to be kept for more than 4 hours before serving, do not add salt until just prior to serving. Salt will cause the liquids to separate in time as it sets with the tomatoes.

 Chef's Tip
When alcohol is added to tomato sauce, it changes the structure of the tomato. It produces an entirely different taste and mouth feel even if all the alcohol is allowed to cook out. Though vodka is odorless and colorless, the reason vodka sauce is made is to exploit that basic molecular change from the alcohol.

Variations

Bolognese meat sauce: Add to the finished tomato sauce ¼ cup each of diced carrots and celery. Add 4 ounces (120mL) chicken stock. Add 2 ounces (60mL) ground pork and 2 ounces (60mL) ground beef. Reduce by half.

Tomato coulis: Add to the completed tomato sauce 2 ounces (60mL) red wine, 4 ounces (120mL) chicken stock, 1 sprig thyme, 1 bay leaf. Reduce by half.

Vodka sauce: Add to the completed tomato sauce 2 ounces (60mL) vodka and 2 ounces (60mL) heavy cream. Simmer for 15 minutes.

Regional Variations of Barbeque

Each region of the United States is known for a different style of barbeque. The variations in the sauces can be traced back to the advancements in refrigeration and transportation. Originally, on the eastern coast of North Carolina where Europeans first settled, the sauce was used much more as a preservative high in acids and salts. Then, as refrigeration came about, the acids were reduced and a thicker tomato component was added. You can experience this in a Memphis-style sauce. When sauces started to be sold commercially and shipped long distances, they were concentrated into thick sauces to reduce shipping size, which is how Kansas City–style sauces were derived.

North Carolina sauce: Omit the ketchup from this recipe, and add ¼ cup kosher salt.

Memphis sauce: Combine all ingredients, but do not cook at all.

Kansas City Barbecue Sauce

Kansas City, Missouri, is well known for its unique, flavorful style of barbecue. The ingredients combined in this recipe create a bold, rich sauce you are sure to love.

 1 quart (1L)

 10 minutes

 30 minutes

INGREDIENTS

1½ cups ketchup

1 cup water

½ cup apple cider vinegar

¼ cup dark brown sugar

2 TB. molasses

1 TB. onion powder

1 TB. garlic powder

1 TB. black pepper

1 tsp. celery salt

1 tsp. allspice

1 tsp. cayenne

TOOLS

1-qt. (1L) saucepan

Wooden spoon or high-temperature spatula

1   In a small saucepan over medium heat, combine ketchup, water, cider vinegar, dark brown sugar, molasses, onion powder, garlic powder, black pepper, celery salt, allspice, and cayenne. Stir constantly for 5 minutes.

2   Reduce heat to low and simmer for 20 minutes, stirring occasionally. Sauce should be thick.

3   Allow sauce to cool. Use immediately, or pour into an airtight container and store covered in the refrigerator until ready to use.

soups and stews

In this chapter, you'll learn how to make the three main styles of soups: *broth, cream,* and *purée.* Once you've learned the essential skills for a particular style, you'll be able to adapt the process and make your own recipes. With these basic skills, you'll have a deeper understanding of how to create other new soup and stew recipes.

Soups and Stews Basics

Soups are considered magical by many people. They're what we eat when we're sick, and they warm us in cold weather. In Paris in 1765, Monsieur Boulanger is said to have started the first modern restaurant by serving hearty soups and stews to travelers as a restorative. In fact, the term restorative became "restaurant." And soups and stews started it all.

These elixirs can be broken down into five basic types of soups: broth soups, purée soups, cream soups, regional soups, and stews. Each different type of soup has a standard cooking method. So once you understand the basics of a particular style, you can branch out and try making different soups using the same method.

Broth soups are light and are made without thickeners.

Purée soups are hearty and thickened by puréeing cooked tubers in the soup.

Cream soups are elegant. They're puréed smooth and strained for added shimmer.

Regional soups are called so because they've become traditional to a certain area and usually showcase local ingredients that are left in the soup bowl.

Stews are thick and rich. They're made by first browning tougher cuts of meat, and then cooking them for a long time to extract the gelatin from the meat, making it tender.

 Soup has been a symbol of the health of family and community for many generations.

Beethoven: "Only the pure of heart can make a soup."

Marge Kennedy: "Soup is a lot like a family. Each ingredient enhances the others; each batch has its own characteristics; and it needs time to simmer to reach full flavor."

Maya Angelou: "Whenever something went wrong when I was young, if I had a pimple or my hair broke—my mom would say, 'Sister mine, I's going to make you some soup.' And I really thought the soup would make my pimple go away or my hair stronger."

What Bones Are the Best to Make Stock?

Bones add flavor to stock, but they also add mouth feel. Gelatin comes from the connective tissue (collagen) between joints. As the stock is cooked, the collagen begins to melt when the temperatures reach 160°F (71°C). As long as the temperature of the stock doesn't get above 208°F (98°C), you'll be dissolving collagen and making gelatin, which will greatly enhance the mouth feel of the stock.

Ideally, the bones you use should have a lot of joints to provide the collagen. Back bones are ideal because they have a lot of joints and contain a lot of meat. This is true with all types of stocks, but bones from other parts of the animal will also add great flavor.

At times, you may not have stock made up and stored and may need to buy a canned broth, a paste base, or a powdered bouillon. When choosing which of these to use, look at the list of ingredients. The first ingredient should be the meat it's made from. Be leery of buying items where the meat is listed after salts and sugars. There are some great products out there; just beware of what you buy.

1 gallon

 10 minutes

 5 hours

INGREDIENTS

1 gal. + 1 qt. (1L) water

7 lbs. (3kg) chicken bones

1 lb. (450g) mirepoix

    ½ lb. (225g) onions, chopped

    ½ lb. (225g) carrots, chopped

    ¼ lb. (113g) celery, chopped

1 sachet d'épices

    1 bay leaf

    2 stems parsley

    1 clove garlic, crushed

    5 whole black peppercorns

    1 tsp. thyme leaves

TOOLS

4-oz. (120mL) ladle

1½-gallon stock pot

Fine-mesh strainer

White Chicken Stock

Chicken stock is the foundation of flavor for many dishes, from sauces to soups, so always take care to produce a good quality stock. With chicken stock, you should have a liquid that smells like chicken but has a neutral flavor. The seasoning will be adjusted when the stock is used.

1 Fill the pot with the water and place it on high temperature. Put the bones in the pot (fig. a). Bring the pot to a boil at 212°F (100°C), and immediately turn down to simmer at 180 to 210°F (82° to 99°C).

2 Simmer 3 hours, skimming the foam and oil from the top every 15 minutes (fig. b). Never mix a stock while it cooks, this will cause it to come out cloudy and have a slightly bitter taste.

3 Add the mirepoix and sachet d'épices (fig. c). Allow it to simmer for an additional 15 minutes.

4 Strain the liquid and discard the solids (fig. d).

If the stock isn't going to be used right away, chill it down in the next 4 hours to below 45°F (7°C) and pour into a storage container. Otherwise, bacterial growth could make it inedible.

 Making Stock in a Pressure Cooker
To make a white stock in a pressure cooker, just add all the ingredients and seal it. At 15 psi (1.5kg/cm), it will take only 20 minutes to cook. With brown stock, brown all the ingredients, add them to the pot, and seal. Cook 1 hour at 15 psi (1.5kg/cm) and you're all set.

Chef's Tip

If you put the bones in the pot and then add the water, you can end up with bones burning on the bottom of the pot. By starting the water on the stove first and then adding the bones, a layer of warm water pushes the hollow poultry bones upward and away from the bottom of the pot.

SOUPS AND STEWS

Brown Beef Stock

Brown stock is much richer than white stock, and less about the neutral flavors and much more about the over-all richness from developing natural sugars and acids. You still need to make sure only the highest-quality ingredients go into the pot.

 1 gallon

 30 minutes

 8 hours

INGREDIENTS

2 oz. (60mL) vegetable oil

1 lb. (450g) mirepoix

  ½ lb. (225g) onions, chopped

  ¼ lb. (113g) carrots, chopped

  ¼ lb. (113g) celery, chopped

2 TB. tomato paste

1½ gal. water

¼ cup red wine vinegar

1 sachet d'épices

  1 bay leaf

  2 stems parsley

  1 clove garlic, crushed

  5 whole black pep-percorns

  1 tsp. thyme leaves

1 Preheat the oven to 400°F (204°C). Place the bones on a sheet pan in the oven (fig. a). Be sure to use a sturdy but old pan, or the high temps will cause it to warp. Cook 20 minutes so the bones and the meat start to turn a rich brown color.

2 Combine oil, onions, and carrots in the pot and set on medium heat (fig. b). Allow to cook, mixing every 4-5 minutes. You're ready for the next step when the onions are completely brown and the carrots are starting to brown.

3 Add celery and tomato paste to the pot (fig. c). Continue to cook on medium until the paste changes from red to an orange color. You'll need to keep slowly mixing and scraping the bottom of the pot, or the sugars in the paste will burn.

4 Add the water and bring it to a simmer. When the bones have browned, remove them from the oven and put them in the liquid (fig. d). Ladle 8 ounces (240mL) of the liquid onto the sheet pan the bones were on. Add the vinegar and scrape (fig. e), then pour this into the stock pot.

5 Simmer 7 hours, skimming the fats and solids from the top every 15 minutes for the first hour. After 7 hours, add the sachet ingredients. Simmer 15 additional minutes and strain through a fine mesh strainer (fig. f). Keep the liquid brown stock and discard the solids.

If the stock isn't going to be used right away, chill it down in the next 4 hours to below 45°F (7°C) and pour into a storage container. Otherwise, bacterial growth could make it inedible.

TOOLS

2-gal. stock pot

4-oz. (120mL) ladle

Fine mesh strainer

Wooden spoon

Spatula

4

 20 minutes

 20 minutes

INGREDIENTS

2 oz. (60mL) vegetable oil

1 lb. (450g) mirepoix

  ½ lb. (225g) onions, chopped

  ¼ lb. (113g) carrots, chopped

  ¼ lb. (113g) celery, chopped

1 clove garlic, minced

1 cup chicken, cooked, small diced

1 qt. (1L) white chicken stock

¼ lb. (113g) noodles

1 sachet d'épices

  1 bay leaf

  2 stems of parsley

  1 clove garlic, crushed

  5 whole black peppercorns

  1 tsp. thyme leaves

2 tsp. kosher salt

½ tsp. black pepper

TOOLS

2-qt. (2L) sauce pot
4-oz. (120mL) ladle
Wooden spoon

Chicken Noodle Soup

Chicken soup is the ultimate comfort food. It's often considered the cure for a cold or a bad day. This recipe is very easy to make, but the most important ingredient here is the stock—if it isn't good quality, your soup will not be a success.

1 Using the oil, sweat the mirepoix until the onions become translucent (fig. a).

2 Add the garlic and chicken (fig. b). Allow it to cook until you can smell the garlic.

3 Add the stock and bring it to a boil. Skim any oil from the top. As soon as the stock comes to a boil, add the noodles and sachet (fig. c).

4 Simmer 12 minutes. Skim any oil and foam from the top again. Mix and adjust seasoning.

Serve immediately, or chill below 45°F (7°C) within 4 hours.

Chicken schmaltz is the oil from the meat. If you save the oil as it floats to the top of the stock, you can use it in place of vegetable oil in your chicken-based recipes. Using chicken schmaltz in this recipe instead of vegetable oil would produce a much richer and even more comforting soup.

a
b
c

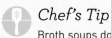 ### Chef's Tip

Broth soups don't contain thickeners, and are garnished with their own ingredients. They're quick cooking and provide a comforting feel. The directions for any broth soup will break down into three basic steps: 1) sweat the flavor ingredients, 2) add the stock and simmer, and 3) season and serve.

SOUPS AND STEWS

Vegetable Beef Soup

Like chicken noodle, this is a broth soup. It's made with the same three basic steps: 1) sweat the flavor ingredients, 2) simmer, and 3) season. Because the beef is a tougher cut of meat, we cook it longer so the connective tissues break down and the meat becomes more tender.

 4

 20 minutes

 1¹/₂ hours

1 Place the pot over high heat. Using the oil, brown the meat to caramelize all sides of the stew meat (fig. a).

2 Turn down the heat to medium. Sweat the mirepoix until the onions become translucent (fig. b).

3 Add the garlic and allow to cook until you can smell the garlic (fig. c).

4 Add the stock and bring it to a boil, then turn the heat down to simmer. Skim any oil and foam from the top.

5 After 1 hour, add the sachet, tomatoes, and corn (fig. d).

6 Simmer 15 minutes. Skim any oil and foam from the top again. Stir and adjust seasoning (fig e.).

Serve immediately or chill below 45°F (7°C) within 4 hours.

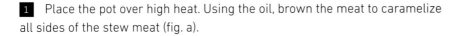 *Essential Technique: Caramelizing*

Caramelization occurs when the sugars in an ingredient are transformed into caramel by applying heat. This can only happen in the absence of water, and care must be taken to control the temperature when caramelizing meats and vegetables to prevent burning. In this recipe, the onions, carrots, and celery are caramelized at medium high heat.

INGREDIENTS

2 oz. (60mL) vegetable oil

1 cup beef stew meat, small diced

1 lb. (450g) mirepoix

   ½ lb. (225g) onions, chopped

   ¼ lb. (113g) carrots, chopped

   ¼ lb. (113g) celery, chopped

1 clove garlic, minced

1 qt. (1L) brown beef stock

¼ cup canned diced tomato

¼ cup corn kernels

1 sachet d'épices

   1 bay leaf

   2 stems of parsley

   1 clove garlic, crushed

   5 whole black peppercorns

   1 tsp. thyme leaves

2 tsp. kosher salt

½ tsp. black pepper

TOOLS

2-qt. (2L) sauce pot

Tongs

4-oz. (120mL) ladle

Wooden spoon

4

 20 minutes

 40 minutes

INGREDIENTS

2 oz. (60mL) corn oil

1 butternut squash

1 tart apple, such as
Granny Smith, peeled,
cored, diced

1 qt. (1L) apple cider

1 sachet d'épices

   5 pink peppercorns

   1 tsp. thyme leaves

   1 bay leaf

   1 clove garlic, minced

   2 cardamom pods

2 cups coconut milk

Kosher salt and white
pepper to taste

TOOLS

Microwave oven

Kitchen spoon

2-qt. (2L) sauce pot

Immersion blender

Butternut Squash Soup

Purée soups are rich, hearty soups that are sometimes served as entrées. All purée soups follow these three steps: 1) combine ingredients, which include a starchy food, 2) add a liquid and simmer ingredients until tender, and 3) purée, season, and serve.

1 Cut the butternut squash in half and remove seeds. Place pulp side down on a plate and rub outside with oil. Place in the microwave for 12 minutes.

2 Remove the pulp from the squash by placing a kitchen spoon between the skin and pulp. Chop into pieces smaller than ½ inch (1.25cm).

3 Combine squash in a large sauce pot with all ingredients through the sachet d'épices. Bring to simmer over medium heat for 20 minutes.

4 Remove sachet and discard. Purée soup with a hand (immersion) blender. Add the coconut milk while puréeing.

Season to taste. Serve immediately or chill below 45°F (7°C) within 4 hours.

 Chef's Tip
By following the steps in this recipe, you can make a purée soup from almost anything.

SOUPS AND STEWS

Chicken Velvet Soup

Cream soups are smooth and delicate, and leave you feeling contemplative and satisfied. The heavy cream used in this recipe makes a smooth, rich dish.

 4

 20 minutes

 20 minutes

1 Using the oil, sweat the mirepoix until the onions become translucent (fig. a).

2 Add the garlic and chicken and allow to cook until you can smell the garlic (fig. b).

3 Add the velouté (fig. c). Bring it to a boil and add the sachet. Skim any oil and foam from the top.

4 Simmer 15 minutes. Skim any oil and foam from the top again. Remove the sachet.

5 Remove from the stove. Add the heavy cream (fig. d). Purée with the hand blender until there are no lumps (fig. e).

6 Strain through a fine-mesh strainer (fig. f). Reheat the soup. Season to taste with salt and white pepper.

Serve immediately or chill below 45°F (7°C) within 4 hours.

 Chef's Tip
The basic steps for making any cream soup are:

1. Combine flavor ingredients.
2. Add stock and thickener and simmer.
3. Purée the soup.
4. Strain the soup.
5. Season and serve.

Many recipes are labeled as cream soups, but in reality most fall into the purée soup category.

INGREDIENTS

2 oz. (60mL) vegetable oil

1 lb. (450g) mirepoix
  ½ lb. (225g) onions, chopped
  ¼ lb. (113g) carrots, chopped
  ¼ lb. (113g) celery, chopped

1 clove garlic, minced

1 cup chicken, cooked, small diced

1 quart chicken velouté

1 sachet d'épices
  1 bay leaf
  2 stems parsley
  1 clove garlic, crushed
  5 whole black peppercorns
  1 tsp. thyme leaves

1 cup heavy cream

2 tsp. kosher salt

½ tsp. white pepper

TOOLS

2-qt. (2L) sauce pot

4-oz. (120mL) ladle

Immersion blender

Large mixing bowl

Fine-mesh strainer

Wooden spoon

4

 20 minutes

 20 minutes

INGREDIENTS

2 slices bacon, small diced

1 oz. (30mL) vegetable oil

½ cup russet potatoes, peeled, small diced

½ cup red potatoes, peeled, small diced

1 TB. whole butter

½ cup onions, small diced

½ cup celery, small diced

¼ cup flour

1 qt. (1L) clam juice

2 tsp. thyme leaves

1 bay leaf

3 cups whole milk

½ cup clams, canned, cut

1 cup heavy cream

Sea salt to taste

White pepper to taste

Worcestershire sauce to taste

Chile pepper hot sauce to taste

TOOLS

2-qt. (2L) sauce pot

High-temperature rubber spatula

4-oz. (120mL) ladle

Wooden spoon

New England Clam Chowder

Chowders are soups that contain pieces of potato. The liquid may change, and the seafood might change or even not be included, but the cooking process is the same and the potatoes are always present. This recipe is for traditional New England–style clam chowder.

1 Put the vegetable oil in the pot with the bacon and cook it on high heat for 4 minutes to render the fat out of the bacon. Add the potatoes and cook 3 more minutes. Turn down the heat to medium. Add the butter, onions, and celery. Cook until the onions are translucent (fig. a).

2 Add the flour to the pot and make a blond roux with the oil and vegetables (fig. b).

3 Stir in the clam juice with the roux and vegetables to make a velouté. Add the bay leaf and thyme (fig. c).

4 Bring to a simmer until the potatoes are tender, about 20 minutes.

5 Add the juice from the canned clams, milk, and heavy cream. Return to a simmer. Season to taste with Worcestershire sauce and chile pepper hot sauce. Put a heaping tablespoon of the clams in serving bowls.

6 Pour the simmering soup over the clams. The soup will be hot enough to cook the clams without making them too tough to eat.

a

b

c

SOUPS AND STEWS

Regional Variations of Chowder

The basic cooking process for chowders is: 1) combine the non-seafood ingredients, 2) simmer to cook the potatoes, and 3) add the seafood and season.

By definition, all chowders contain potatoes. But chowders come in many forms. In New England, they're thick and creamy with big clams. In New York, a tomato-based liquid is used instead of dairy. Farther down the East Coast are broth chowders without dairy or tomatoes. In the Midwest, you'll find corn in the chowder, but no seafood. Wherever you are, though, the chowder comes with potatoes.

In this recipe, you can exchange Béchamel for tomato sauce to make New York clam chowder, or add fish velouté to make Maryland clam chowder.

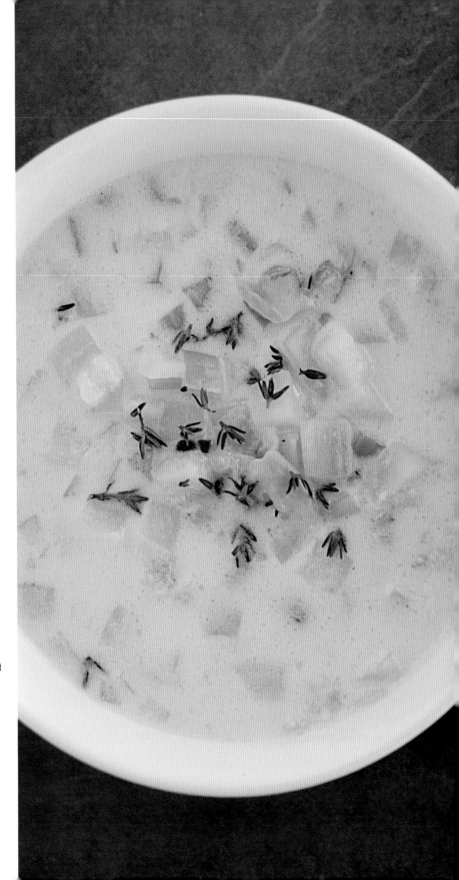

Variations

By making a couple of changes in this basic stewing recipe, you can make a variety of different stews that will keep you warm through the winter.

Lamb Stew: Replace the beef with lamb stew meat.

Braised Shank: Replace the meat in this recipe with beef or lamb shanks.

Yankee Pot Roast: Use a chuck steak instead of diced beef.

Beef Stew

Stewing relies on controlling the temperature of the liquid in which the main food is cooked. In this recipe, you learn the basic steps of making a stew. Once you're familiar with this recipe, you can try different ingredients to make variations.

 4

 20 minutes

 1½ hours

INGREDIENTS

2 lb. (1kg) beef chuck, boneless

1 TB. salt

1 tsp. pepper

2 oz. (60mL) vegetable oil

1 onion, finely diced

2 cloves garlic, chopped

2 oz. (60mL) flour

2 oz. (60mL) tomato purée

1 qt. (1L) brown stock

1 bay leaf

Pinch dried thyme

1 loaf French bread, 1-inch (2.5cm) slices

1　Cut beef into 1-inch cubes and mix with salt and pepper. Cut all pieces of meat the same size. If they're different sizes, they won't cook at the same rate. Heat the oil in a pot on high heat until very hot. Sear all sides of the meat. Remove and continue the process until all the meat is browned (fig. a).

2　Turn the heat down to medium. In the same pan, add the onions to the meat and continue to cook until onion is lightly browned, stirring slowly. Add the garlic and flour. The flour and oil will combine to make a roux that will thicken the stew as it cooks. Add the tomato purée (fig. b). Continue to cook over medium heat for 3 minutes.

3　Turn the heat back to high. With a wooden spoon, stir until all the flour lumps are gone. Pour the stock into the pot (fig. c). Bring the mixture to a boil and immediately turn down the heat as the sauce thickens.

4　Add the bay leaf and thyme. Cover the pot and place in the oven (fig. d) at 250°F (120°C). Let it cook in the oven without looking for 1½-2 hours. Check to see if the meat is tender by putting a fork straight down into a piece and lifting the fork straight back up. If the meat falls off the fork, it is fork tender and ready to eat.

5　Remove the bay leaf and adjust salt and pepper to your taste. Spoon off any grease on the top. Ladle the stew into a bowl and serve with crusty French bread.

TOOLS

Bread knife

Portion scale

6-qt. (6L) pot

Wooden spoon

6-oz. (180mL) ladle

4

 20 minutes

 1 hour

INGREDIENTS

2 oz. (60mL) vegetable oil

1 lb. (450g) ground beef

1 cup onions, small diced

1 clove garlic, minced

2 tablespoons chili
powder

2 cans kidney beans

2 cans crushed tomatoes

1 can tomato juice

2 cups brown beef sauce

1 bay leaf

2 tsp. kosher salt

½ tsp. white pepper

TOOLS

2-qt. (2L) sauce pot

High-temperature rubber
spatula

4-oz. (120mL) ladle

Beef Chili

There are many different opinions on what ingredients chili should contain. Many cooks don't use meat; others think it should never have beans. I personally believe good chili should include beans, so I use kidney beans in this recipe.

1 Brown the meat in oil in a very hot pot over high heat.

2 Turn down the temperature to medium. Add the onions to the pot with the meat and cook until they're translucent. Add the garlic and chili powder. Cook until you can smell the powder starting to toast, about 1 minute.

3 Add the kidney beans, tomato products, brown sauce, and bay leaf and simmer for 1 hour.

4 Serve the chili with your favorite toppings.

 Chef's Tip
Note that the chili powder needs to be added to oil in order for it to dissolve. Many of the spices in chili powder are oil soluble, not water soluble. If you add the powder after the liquids have been added, you'll be left with a gritty texture from the undissolved chili powder.

SOUPS AND STEWS

salads

In this chapter, you'll learn the four parts of a salad and how to alter them to make your own fantastic and unique salads. You'll also explore the different types of lettuces and greens, the various flavors that can be conjured from them, and how you can take your salads from mundane to spectacular.

Salad Basics

The word "salad" actually derives from "salt." Originally, salads were nothing more than greens that were salted and spritzed with a lemon to make them come alive. They were served after an entrée to refresh the diner's palate before the service of sweets. Today, salads come in all forms, from lettuces to meats, from potatoes to grains.

It's very important to remember the role the salad plays in the meal. Until the last 50 years, salads were served after the entrée and were lively in acid. Today, many people serve salads before the entrée to give guests more time to finish the main course. If it's served before an entrée, much care must be taken to ensure the intensity of the salad course doesn't overpower the entrée. Richer, heavier salads could easily stick to the palate, so think light, crisp flavors when preparing this course.

If it's a formal party, a composed salad would be in favor. With a composed salad, every component has a specific location on the plate. Greens, such as lettuce stems, are arranged in an orderly fashion and there is a clear flow between the foods. On the other hand, informal family dinners may be much simpler, with the greens and other ingredients piled unarranged on the plate and then covered with a dressing. Each of these styles has its place.

Anatomy of a Salad

Salads have four parts to them: *base, body, garnish,* and *dressing.*

The base is often just a whole lettuce leaf that lies in the bottom of the bowl. It's a different color so that it forms a frame around the body of the salad. The base also allows extra water or dressing to go under it so you won't eat soggy lettuce leaves.

The body is the naming factor for most salads. For instance, the body of a chicken salad is chicken.

The garnish is an item that brings taste, texture, and/or color that would be missing otherwise.

Finally, the dressing does a few things. It adds taste to balance the flavors of the body element. The dressing should enhance the body, not overpower it. The vinegar in the dressing helps break down some items in lettuces that would not digest otherwise. The oil in the vinaigrette helps dissolve oil-soluble vitamins and make them more digestible. The four parts of any salad work together to make it look and taste great.

Types of Salad Greens

Greens for salads fall into three main categories: *head lettuce, loose leaf,* and *coles.* A combination of the three is often used to add interest and depth of flavors.

Head lettuces include icebergs, romaines, and butter heads. They grow to form overlapping leaves that will hold together. Loose leaf is a broad range of lettuces that grow in single stems and leaves and include oak leaf, mache, arugula, and chicory. The last category is the coles, which are more densely leaved greens that have a very strong, bitter flavor. These would include cabbages, mustards, collards, and kale.

Head lettuce	*Loose leaf*	*Cole*

Buying Greens

When buying salad greens, look for firm leaves that stand up on their own. They shouldn't be kept under a water system in the grocery store, as this increases the likelihood that they will have bad bacteria growing on them.

In an ideal world, you would purchase lettuces directly from a farmer at a market. In those cases you will most likely be able to taste them before you buy them. The flavor of a fresh piece of lettuce grown in rich soils is dramatically different from lettuces grown in mass and shipped across the continent. Like most fruits and vegetables, they start losing nutritional value the day they're picked, so in an ideal world you would be getting them grown close to home and picked the same day.

Storing Greens

Greens need moisture and the right temperatures to stay fresh. They should be wrapped in moist paper towels and stored in the refrigerator at 34° to 40°F (1° to 4.5°C). If they fall below freezing, the water in the lettuce will freeze, ruining the structure, so be careful not to store them in a part of the refrigerator that might blow cold air on them.

Cleaning Greens

Lettuces should be cleaned when they're ready to be used, not when or before you've purchased them. Quality-grown produce have natural beneficial bacteria that keep them from aging or growing bad bacteria. When this is washed off, the product will go bad within hours or days. The water you use to wash the produce also acts as an accelerator for many bad bacteria.

When you're ready to use lettuces, pull off and discard the outer leaves; the rest of the leaves can be pulled apart and used. Place lettuce leaves in a sink full of clean and very cold water. Mix them around and let them sit in the water for several minutes. All the dirt should fall to the bottom of the sink and the leaves should float to the top. Carefully remove the leaves from the water so the dirt stays in the sink. Repeat this process until you don't see any more dirt in the bottom of the sink after the leaves are removed.

4

 5 minutes

 none

INGREDIENTS

4 outer radicchio leaves

4 oz. mesclun mix salad
  greens

4 oz. salad dressing

8 red cherry tomatoes, cut
  in half lengthwise

8 yellow cherry tomatoes,
  cut in half lengthwise

TOOLS

Scale

Mixing bowl

Tongs

Basic Garden Salad

Garden salads are a staple of many meals. They usually
reflect what is in season in the garden. These salads
are most often served between courses to cleanse
the palate.

1 Place the outer radicchio leaves cup
side up in the bottom of a salad bowl
(fig. a).

2 Place 4 ounces (110g) of greens into
a mixing bowl. Add 4 ounces (120mL)
of dressing. Using tongs, carefully toss
the salad until all the greens are evenly
coated with dressing (fig. b).

3 Place ¼ of the mix into each of four
radicchio cups.

4 Garnish each salad with 4 red cherry
tomato halves (fig. c) and 4 yellow tomato
halves. Serve immediately. If a salad has
dressing on it, it will last only about 15
minutes until the acid in the dressing
causes the greens to wilt.

a

b

c

 Chef's Note

If you remember the 3 part oil to 1 part vinegar ratio, you can make
most any dressing you desire. To make basic balsamic vinaigrette,
blend 1 part balsamic vinegar with 3 parts olive oil finished with salt,
pepper, and herbs. You can change the vinegar and oil to whatever
types you want.

Chef's Note
The traditional Caesar dressing is prepared in a wooden bowl next to the dining room table. The way most servers remember to mix everything together is to mix in order of color from lightest to darkest. This way, the dressing stays emulsified and the flavors can best be adjusted.

Caesar Salad

Caesar salad was first made by Caesar Cardini on a busy July 4th weekend in 1924. Caesar's restaurant had run out of many things, so Caesar grabbed what he had and made this salad in front of everyone in the dining room. It was an instant success.

1   In the blender, place anchovies, mustard, garlic, lemon juice, egg, cheese, salt, and pepper. Run the blender just long enough to incorporate all the ingredients together (fig. a).

2   With the blender running, pour the oil in slowly (fig. b).

3   Place the whole romaine leaves on serving bowls. In the mixing bowl, place the torn romaine. Add the dressing and toss so it's evenly incorporated (fig. c). Put ¼ of the mix into each of four salad bowls on top of the lettuce leaves.

4   Garnish each salad with 6 Parmesan seasoned bread crumbs (fig. d). Serve immediately. If a salad has dressing on it, it will last only about 15 minutes until the acid in the dressing causes the greens to wilt.

 4

 10 minutes

 none

DRESSING INGREDIENTS

2 anchovy filets

1 tsp. dry mustard powder

1 clove garlic, chopped

1 TB. lemon juice

1 egg yolk

1 oz. (29g) grated Parmesan cheese

1 tsp. sea salt

½ tsp. fresh ground black pepper

9 oz. (270mL) olive oil, not extra virgin

SALAD INGREDIENTS

4 whole romaine leaves

8 oz. (225g) romaine leaves, cleaned, torn into 1-inch (2.5cm) strips

6 oz. (180mL) Caesar dressing

24 Parmesan seasoned bread crumbs

TOOLS

Blender

Mixing bowl

Tongs

4

 20 minutes

 none

DRESSING INGREDIENTS

½ tsp. brown sugar

1 tsp. sea salt

½ tsp. black pepper

½ tsp. Worcestershire sauce

¼ tsp. dry mustard powder

1 clove garlic, minced

1 tsp. lemon juice

¼ cup red wine vinegar

¼ cup extra virgin olive oil

¾ cup vegetable oil

SALAD INGREDIENTS

½ head shredded iceberg lettuce

1 bunch watercress, cleaned

1 bunch chicory (or baby arugula), cleaned

½ head romaine, cleaned and torn into 1-inch (2.5cm) strips

2 plum tomatoes, seeds removed

4 strips bacon, cooked, crumbled

2 chicken breasts, cooked and medium diced

2 boiled eggs, shelled and chopped

1 avocado, small diced, tossed in lemon juice

½ cup Roquefort cheese, crumbled

2 TB. chives

TOOLS

Blender

Mixing bowl

Tongs

Cobb Salad

Late at night in the famous Brown Derby restaurant in Hollywood, owner Bob Cobb needed a snack, so he went into the cooler, grabbed some ingredients, and created a magical salad that he presented to his customers. The next night they started coming in asking for *Cobb's salad*.

1 In the blender, combine brown sugar, sea salt, black pepper, Worcestershire sauce, dry mustard powder, garlic, lemon juice, and red wine vinegar. Pulse it on and off until incorporated (fig. a).

2 With the blender running, pour in the two oils. Turn the blender off, pour the oils into a storage container, and chill for service.

3 Place a base of shredded iceberg lettuce in the bottom of each of four salad bowls. In the mixing bowl, combine watercress, chicory or baby arugula, and romaine. Toss with 6 ounces (180mL) of the dressing made above (fig. b).

4 Place ¼ of the dressed lettuces in each salad bowl. Top with a line of each of the garnishes (fig. c). Serve immediately.

SALADS

　　　　　　　　　　　SALADS

Kale Salad

Greens are a staple food in many parts of the world. They're nutritionally dense and grow well in cool or hot climates, so it's important to know how to clean and use this versatile green. In this recipe you'll learn the quick way of folding and cutting out the fibrous stem, which needs to be removed, as it is not easily edible.

 4

 10 minutes

 20 minutes

INGREDIENTS

1 bunch kale

¼ cup lemon juice

¼ cup extra virgin olive oil

¼ cup pecan pieces

¼ cup raisins

½ cup bourbon whiskey

4 large red kale leaves

1 tsp. sea salt

¼ tsp. ground black pepper

TOOLS

Sheet pan

Small sauce pot

1 Rinse kale thoroughly, making sure all the sand has been rinsed from the leaves. Fold the kale in half along the stem. Use a knife to cut along the stem and remove it (fig. a). Once the stems have been removed, chiffonade the leaves into ½ inch (1.25cm) strips. Work the lemon juice all around the kale leaves. Then toss them in the olive oil. Allow to marinate together (fig. b).

2 Place the nuts on a sheet pan and put them in a 300°F (150°C) oven for 4 minutes. Remove and allow to cool to room temperature.

3 Place the raisins and bourbon in a small sauce pot (fig. c). Put on the stove at medium heat and allow to cook until the liquid begins to boil. Remove from the heat and allow to rest for 15 minutes. (You'll notice the raisins plump up.) Drain the bourbon off the raisins.

4 In the bottom of each of four bowls, place the red kale leaves. Place the marinated kale on top. Garnish with the nuts and plumped raisins (fig. d). Finish with salt and pepper.

4

 20 minutes

 none

DRESSING INGREDIENTS

1 cup mayonnaise (see recipe in the Sauces and Condiments chapter)

1 TB. apple cider vinegar

¼ tsp. Worcestershire sauce

½ TB. kosher salt

1 tsp. large-grind black pepper

1 TB. honey

BODY INGREDIENTS

4 cups shredded cabbage

1 carrot, shredded

1 onion, shredded

1 red pepper, julienned

10 cilantro leaves, chopped

TOOLS

2 mixing bowls

Whisk

Box grater

Food processor with slicing and shredding attachments (optional)

Cole Slaw

Cole slaw is a staple of backyard barbeques. It's tangy and helps clear the palate of the spice and sweetness of the barbeque. The key to this recipe is to cut the cabbage thin. You can use your choice of cabbage: green, purple, Napa, or Chinese.

1 Combine all the dressing ingredients (fig. a). Put into the refrigerator to chill while the rest of the recipe is prepared.

2 Remove any outer cabbage leaves that are damaged or dirty. Cut the cabbage into quarters from the stem end to the top.

3 Cut the core out of the cabbage by cutting at an angle out from the stem to the end of the thick white leaves near the middle.

4 Chiffonade the cabbage ¼ inch (6.5mm) thick (fig. b). This can be done by hand or using a slicing attachment on a food processor.

5 Using a box grater or a food processor with a shredding attachment, peel and shred the carrot and onion.

6 Combine all the body ingredients in a bowl and toss (fig. c). Add the dressing at the desired consistency to the point the dressing evenly coats the cabbage and binds all the ingredients together. Lay the slaw over a bed of sliced red pepper and garnish with cilantro.

a

b

c

Chicken Salad

The chicken in this classic recipe can easily be substituted to make a seafood salad, as well. For a salmon salad, simply use salmon instead of chicken and keep all the other ingredients the same.

 4

 20 minutes

 15 minutes

INGREDIENTS

1 lb. (450g) chicken breasts, boneless, skinless

1 TB. sea salt

½ tsp. white pepper

2 TB. olive oil

¼ cup mayonnaise (see recipe in the Sauces and Condiments chapter)

1 TB. curry powder

¼ cup grapes, cut in half

¼ cup pecan pieces

2 TB. fresh tarragon, chopped

4 leaves romaine lettuce

TOOLS

Sheet pan

Meat thermometer

Mixing bowl

1 Preheat the oven to 250°F (120°C). Place chicken breasts on a sheet pan. Season with salt and pepper (this may seem like a lot of salt, but when mixed into the final salad the salt will be much more spread out). Spread olive oil on both sides of the breasts. Place the sheet pan in the oven for 12 minutes.

2 After 12 minutes, remove the pan from the oven and immediately check the temperature of the breasts with the meat thermometer. (Do this by sticking the end through the thin side and at least 2 inches (5cm) into the meat.) Let the thermometer stay inside the chicken for 30 seconds before reading the temperature gauge. If it's at least 162°F (72°C), turn off the oven and remove the chicken. If it's not at 162°F (72°C) yet, return the pan to the oven for another 5 minutes. Continue this process until they reach 165°F (72°C).

3 Place the chicken breasts into the freezer to cool. Combine all ingredients except the chicken and romaine lettuce in a mixing bowl. Fully incorporate all ingredients.

4 When the chicken has cooled to 40°F (4.5°C) , dice it into a medium dice. Toss the chicken with the other mixed ingredients. Taste for proper seasoning.

5 Put the romaine lettuce in a salad bowl. Top with a scoop of the salad. This salad could also be served on bread or a croissant as a sandwich

 It's essential that chicken used in this recipe be cooked to 165°F (75°C). This is the temperature at which all the bacteria that can make you sick is killed off. The chicken then must be cooled down below 40°F (4.5°C) so that no new bacterial growth occurs. If it's not chilled below 40°F (4.5°C) before the dressing is added, the bacteria can grow quickly from the mayonnaise. Follow the chicken cooking and cooling steps closely. If it's overcooked, the chicken will become dry.

beef and pork

In this chapter, you'll learn three of the core cooking techniques every cook should know: *sautéing, braising,* and *grilling.* Sautéing and grilling are methods that combine quick cooking and bright flavors. Braising takes a bit longer, but it gives your dishes rich and complex flavors. This chapter will help you develop a more complete understanding of the foods you cook.

How to Buy and Store Meats

Meat makes up the biggest part of most people's diet. It's also one thing most new cooks fear cooking, but if you understand a few basics, you can tackle this job easily.

When you purchase meats, consider how you're going to cook them. Meats fall into two categories, tough cuts and tender cuts. Tough cuts come from the parts of the animal that get the most exercise, which include muscle strands that have lots of connective tissue, called *collagen*. You'll need to cook these cuts longer using one of the moist-heat cooking methods—simmering, stewing, braising, and smoking. Tender cuts come from the least-used muscles, which are usually long muscle strands with little collagen. These make great steaks and roasts, and they're best cooked using dry-heat cooking methods—grilling, sautéing, deep frying, and roasting.

The USDA oversees the slaughter and grading of meat. Inspectors check to see how healthy the animal was, how much fat there is in the meat, and if the meat has been aged, but the biggest factor in the grading is intramuscular fat, called *marbling*. The more marbling, the tenderer, juicier, and more flavorful the meat is. The grading is different based on the type of animal, so there are different grading systems between beef and pork, for instance.

Aging is also a major consideration in grading. Meat that is not aged, or not frozen in the first 12 hours, has not gone into rigor mortis. This is called "green" meat, and it's tough and not very flavorful. The longer the meat ages, the more tender it becomes. The aging process can be either "wet aging" or "dry aging." With wet aging, meat is put into a vacuum-sealed bag with chemicals to hasten the process. It's shipped to stores and ages in the few days before it's used. Dry aged meat is kept in a cooler at low humidity. Most meat lovers will tell you meat tastes best when it's dry aged for 21 days.

Meat is 75 percent water, and you want to make sure as much of that water stays in the meat as possible. This is where proper storage comes in. If you store meat wrapped in plastic, the water could become rancid, so it's better to open the ends of the packaging so some air can get in, which increases the shelf life by several days. Even better would be to buy meat from a butcher's counter where it's wrapped in air-permeable paper.

Because meats are potentially hazardous foods, you must take care to store them properly, and near the bottom of the refrigerator. Raw poultry should be kept on the lowest shelf or in a drawer in case it leaks. I store my meat in the crisper drawer of the fridge so if it does leak, it's contained. I can also set the temperature of the drawer a bit lower than the rest of the refrigerator. Meat is best stored between 33° and 40°F (.5° to 4.5°C).

Use meats within four to five days of purchasing or thawing; use ground meats within two to three days. It's best to thaw meats in the refrigerator over several days, and never thaw them by leaving them out at room temperature. This causes the growth of bacteria that could potentially be hazardous.

Beef Basics

The USDA grades beef for sale as *prime, choice, select,* or *standard.*

Prime beef is of the highest quality and marbling. Prime is hard to find, as most of it goes to country clubs and high-end steak houses. (In my opinion, prime is too fatty. The texture becomes too "melt in your mouth" and it doesn't have much of a bite).

Choice is still very high in quality and is preferred by most chefs.

Select will start to get a little tougher and lose more flavor than choice.

Standard is a good pick for tougher cuts of meat used for stewing or braising.

 Properly Sourcing Beef

Looking into the details of where beef comes from can help to fine-tune your flavor preferences. What the animal's breed is and what it eats are the major concerns. Most cattle are raised grazing in fields for the first couple of years of their life, and then are sent to feedlots where they spend another eight months to two years. In the feedlots they're fed a grain-based diet that helps them develop much more marbling and put on overall weight, which helps the owner get a higher price for the animal. This is referred to as *grain-finished* beef. If the animal stays out in the fields and is never brought into the feedlot, it's said to be *grass-finished*. The meat from grass-finished animals is more flavorful and a bit tougher than grain-finished. But note that the terms grain-finished and grass-finished are not regulated at all. It's best to buy beef directly from the farmers whenever possible so they can explain their practices to you.

Basic Beef Cuts

The following chart shows the basic types of beef cuts and where they come from on the cow.

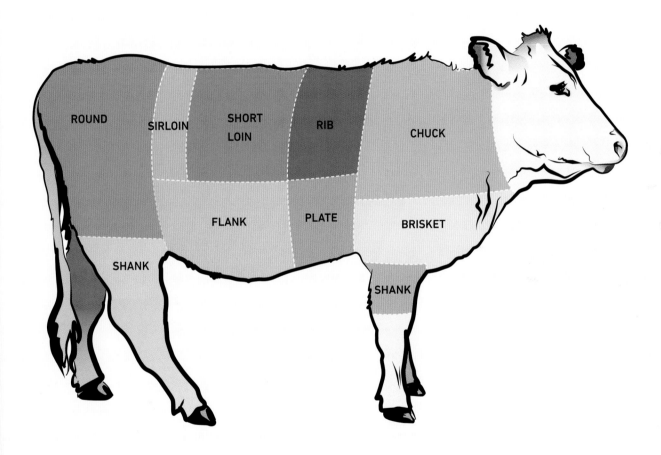

4

 5 minutes

 10-20 minutes

INGREDIENTS

4 (less than 1½-inch [3.75cm] thick) New York strip, T-bone, filet mignon, or porterhouse steaks

2 TB. kosher salt

¼ TB. black pepper

¼ cup vegetable oil

TOOLS

Transport tray

Paper towel

Tongs

Squirt bottle filled with water

Meat thermometer

Serving platter

Basic Grilled Steaks

When I think about grilling out, the first thing I think of is a big, juicy steak. But too often, when I go to a cookout, I get a big, dry steak. If you follow this simple recipe, you'll have people asking for your grilling secrets.

1 Preheat the grill to medium-high. Lay steaks out on the transport tray and blot with a paper towel to remove any wetness.

2 Season both sides of the steaks with kosher salt and black pepper (fig. a). Rub down with vegetable oil, evenly dispersing it, to help conduct the heat from the grill to the steaks.

3 Using tongs, place the steaks on the hottest part of the grill over direct heat, and allow to cook for 2 minutes (fig. b). If flames start to burn up from the bottom of the grill, douse with the squirt bottle.

4 Rotate the steaks 45 degrees to make a cross-hatch pattern, and cook for 2 minutes. If steaks stick to the grill as you're doing this, just wait another minute and then rotate. As they caramelize, they'll stop sticking.

5 Flip the steaks and repeat the process on the other side (fig. c). Put a meat thermometer in the steaks to check doneness (see the following table), making sure at least 1 full inch (2.5 cm) of the thermometer stem is in the meat. Cooking time will vary, depending on thickness and marbling.

6 When the desired temperature is reached, remove the steaks from the grill and place on a serving platter. Let the steaks rest for 5 minutes to allow juices to redistribute evenly.

BEEF AND PORK

a

b

c

How Do You Like Your Steak?

Doneness	Internal Temperature	How It Looks
Rare	125°F (52°C)	
Medium-rare	135°F (57°C)	
Medium	145°F (63°C)	
Medium-well	155°F (68°C)	
Well	165°F (74°C)	

BASIC GRILLED STEAKS

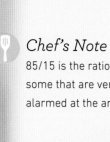

Chef's Note

85/15 is the ratio of lean meat to fat: 85 percent lean meat and 15 percent fat. You can find different ratios, some that are very lean. As the burger cooks, a large percentage of the oils will be drawn out. Don't be alarmed at the amount of fat—this will make a very tender burger.

Hamburgers

Sauté means "to jump" in French. It comes from the action meat makes when put it into a very hot pan. Good lean ground beef and a smoking hot skillet help perfect this classic sautéed hamburger.

 4

 10 minutes

 10 minutes

INGREDIENTS

1 lb. (450g) ground beef 85/15

1 TB. kosher salt

½ tsp. black pepper

2 oz. (60mL) vegetable oil

4 hamburger buns

Condiments of choice

TOOLS

Portion scale

Cast iron skillet

Meat thermometer

1 Portion ground meat into 4 burgers. Work the meat as little as possible. The more you form and press the meat, the more compact the finished product. Pressing lightly between your palms works best.

2 Season both sides of the meat with salt and pepper, and coat both sides with oil. Preheat the skillet over high heat. Make sure there's nothing else near the skillet, the oil will splatter as the burgers cook (and that's a good sign).

3 When you see the skillet start to smoke, put in the burgers. The surface should never be more than ¾ filled. This helps the skillet regain heat as the cold patties are put in. You'll probably need to cook the burgers in two batches. Cook the burgers on this side for 2 minutes.

4 Turn the burgers onto a part of the skillet that didn't have a burger covering it. Cook for 2 more minutes. Check the temperature by sticking a thermometer in the side with the tip reaching into the middle of the burger. If the temperature is 155°F (75°C) or higher, remove from the skillet. If it's lower than 155°F (75°C), flip again and turn the flame to low. Every 2 minutes, flip the burgers and check the temperature again. When it reaches 155° F (75°C), remove.

Place the hamburgers on buns and serve with your favorite condiments and toppings.

 When you sauté, it's essential to use thin, tender cuts of meat. It's a quick cooking process that doesn't allow thicker cuts to cook, and doesn't provide the moisture needed to break down tougher cuts. The key is to have the pan smoking hot and use just enough oil to coat the bottom of the pan.

4

 20 minutes

 2 ¹⁄₂ hours

INGREDIENTS

2 lb. (1kg) bottom round, boneless, trimmed and tied

1 TB. kosher salt

1 tsp. pepper

2 oz. (60mL) vegetable oil

1 onion, finely diced

1 carrot, finely diced

2 celery stalks, finely diced

2 cloves garlic, chopped

2 oz. (60mL) flour

2 oz. (60mL) tomato purée

1 qt. (1L) brown stock

1 bay leaf

Pinch dried thyme

TOOLS

Portion scale

6-qt. (6L) pan

Wooden kitchen spoons

6-oz. (180mL) ladle

Pot Roast

Braising produces rich, savory foods that make your mouth water, and pot roast is no exception. This classic braised roast makes me think of cold winter days with the smell of meat wafting through the kitchen.

1   Season the meat with salt and pepper. Heat the oil in a pot on high until hot enough to get a hard sear on the meat.

2   Add the meat to the pan and sear on all sides (fig. a). When the meat is added to the pan it should make a loud searing noise. If it doesn't, remove the meat until the pan is hotter.

3   Turn the heat down to medium. In the same pan, add the onions, carrots, and celery and cook until the onions are lightly browned, stirring slowly (fig. b). Add the garlic and flour and continue to cook for 3 minutes.

4   Turn the heat back to high. With a wooden spoon, pour the tomato purée and stock into the pan. Bring the mixture to a boil and immediately turn the heat down. Stir with a spoon as the sauce thickens and all the flour lumps are gone (fig. c).

5   Add the bay leaf and thyme. Cover the pan and place in the oven at 250°F (120°C) to cook for two hours (do not open the pan during this time). After two hours, check to see if the meat is tender by putting a fork straight down into it and lifting the fork straight back up. If the meat falls off the fork, it's fork tender and ready to eat.

6   Remove the roast and strain the sauce through a colander. Slice the meat and serve drizzled with 2 ounces (60mL) of sauce.

Chef's Note

Braising involves a few essential steps. It starts with browning the meat, then browning the flavoring ingredients in the same pan. Return the meat to the pan along with everything else. Add liquid, cover, and cook for a long period of time without peeking into the pot. When it's fork tender, you remove the meat and strain the sauce.

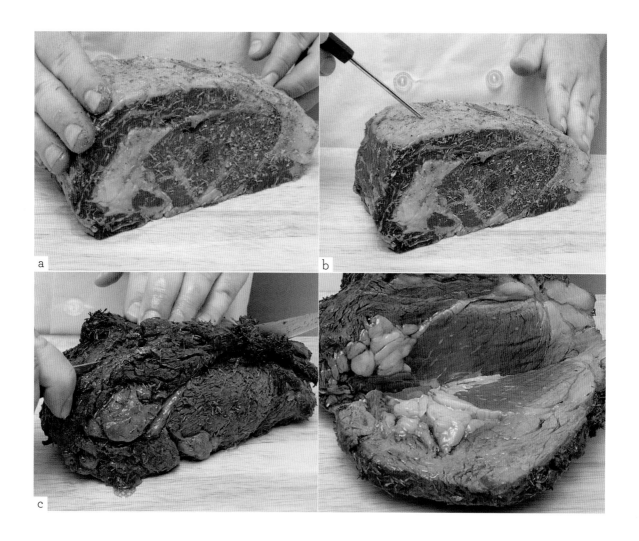

Chef's Tip

Oil foods after you season them, not before. You want to season the food, not the oil. If you oil the food and then season it, the oil creates a barrier to the food, and often the seasonings will just run off the food as it cooks if they're added on top of the oil

BEEF AND PORK

Roast Prime Rib of Beef

 10

 20 minutes

 1½ hours

The basic technique of roasting is to season the food, put it in the oven, and cook to the desired temperature. You must start with a tender cut of meat for this cooking technique. The dry heat actually will cause a tough cut to become even tougher.

INGREDIENTS

5 lb. (2.5kg) prime rib

2 TB. kosher salt

1 TB. black pepper, ground

1 TB. dried thyme leaves

¼ cup vegetable oil

1 Preheat the oven to 425°F (220°C). Place the meat on a sheet pan and dry with paper towels. Season on all sides with salt, pepper, and thyme (fig. a). Rub with oil.

2 Place an in-oven thermometer in the middle of the prime rib (fig. b). Place the prime rib in the oven. Run the in-oven thermometer cord to the receiver. Close the door and turn the heat down to 250°F (120°C).

TOOLS

Sheet pan

In-oven meat thermometer

Serving platter

3 When the prime rib reaches 5 degrees less than your desired doneness, remove from the oven and allow to rest for 20 minutes before carving. In the meantime, pour the pan drippings into a small sauce pot. Skim the oil off the top. Taste and season the remaining drippings, called *au jus*.

4 Slice the meat across the grain in the desired thickness (fig. c). Serve with a coating of au jus.

Chef's Tip

Roasting is a dry-heat cooking method that some call baking. But the main difference between roasting and baking is that roasting is cooking foods that are savory and baking is cooking foods with sugars.

Pork Basics

Pork is the largest-growing category of meat in the world and the meat of choice for most chefs. It's something everyone should know how to cook, and the way some chefs talk about how much they enjoy working with and eating pork gives it a sort of cultish feeling. That trend applies to the general population when it comes to bacon. You can find almost anything that is bacon flavored, from sodas to candies.

Like beef, the slaughter of pork is regulated by the USDA, although USDA grading is not required. If a facility chooses to have the pork graded, it falls into a numbered category of 1 to 4, with 1 being the highest grade. Since the USDA doesn't require grading, many fabrication facilities have started their own grading systems, which are not regulated by the government, and therefore have no true meaning. Look for "USDA" and the number, otherwise it's just a butcher's independent grading system.

Because pork spends most of its life standing and walking around with its weight mostly on its front legs, the areas in and above the front legs contain the toughest and most flavorful meat. The middle back section, called the *loin,* is the least used by the animal. The meats from this area of the animal are usually cut into steaks. Of particular note, the loin and the tenderloin are two different cuts of meat, and the back legs are the fresh hams. The hams can also be tough, but not nearly as tough as the front legs.

Chef's Note

For many years the pork industry tried to breed all the fat out of pigs to make it lean for consumers who were concerned about fat intake. What resulted was meat that was extremely lean but had little taste, and family recipes that called for pork no longer tasted the same. Growers have started going back to a more balanced fat content. If you can find meat from a heritage breed of pig, most of your pork recipes will work and taste better. The best breeds include Berkshire, Duroc, China-Poland, and Mangalitsa.

Basic Pork Cuts

The following chart shows the basic cuts of pork you should know.

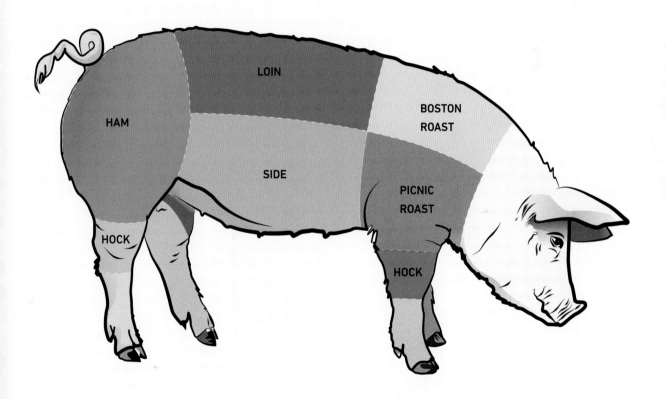

4

 10 minutes

 4 minutes

INGREDIENTS

1 lb. (450g) pork loin

1 TB. kosher salt

1 tsp. black pepper

2 TB. flour

¼ cup vegetable oil

TOOLS

Plastic wrap

Meat mallet

Iron skillet

Tongs

Pork Schnitzel

Pork schnitzel is a thin cut of pork that has been pressed out and sautéed. It's called by many names, depending on the sauce that's served with the dish. In the midwestern United States, it's even served as a sandwich.

1 Cut the meat into 4 pieces. Put a piece of plastic wrap on the tabletop and lay a piece of pork on top of the plastic wrap, then lay another piece of plastic wrap over the pork. Using a meat mallet, pound the meat down to ¼ inch (.5cm) thick (fig. a).

2 Season the meat on both sides with salt and pepper. Flour both sides of the meat (fig. b).

3 Heat the pan with the oil in it until the oil just begins to smoke. Place the pork in the pan (fig. c). Remember not to overcrowd the pan.

4 Cook the pork for 2 minutes on one side, turn, and cook for 2 minutes on the other side (fig. d). Remove from the pan to a plate with a paper towel in order to drain excess oil. Allow to rest for 1 minute.

Finish with sauce of choice, or serve as is.

 Chef's Tip
The technique of pressing out meat by pounding with a mallet can also be used on thin, tender cuts of beef or veal.

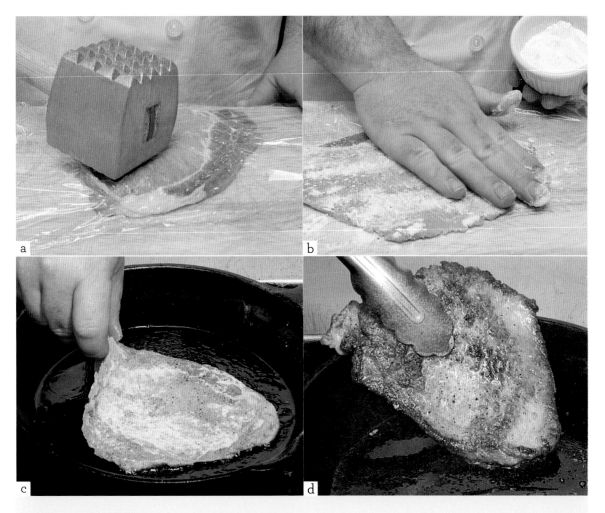

Sauce Variations

Lemon: The traditional version of this dish would be served with just a squeeze of lemon.

White wine: After removing the pork from the pan, remove the pan from the stove and add 2 ounces (60mL) of white wine. Stir to combine pan drippings. Strain onto the pork.

Caper sauce: Use the same recipe as above with 1 tablespoon of capers added to the wine.

Dijon: After removing the pork from the pan, deglaze the pan by adding 2 ounces (60mL) of chicken stock and 2 ounces (60mL) of beef stock. Simmer to reduce by half. Add 1 tablespoon of Dijon mustard.

Grilled Pork Chops

Grilling is a dry-heat cooking process where the food is placed directly over a flame or other heat source. It's best for thin, tender cuts of meat like pork chops. When the heat is above the food, the process is called *broiling*.

 4

 5 minutes

 10 minutes

INGREDIENTS

4 8 oz. (225g) bone-in
 pork chops
2 TB. kosher salt
¼ TB. black pepper
¼ cup vegetable oil

TOOLS

Transport tray
Tongs
Squirt bottle of water
Meat thermometer
Serving platter

a

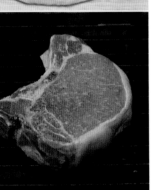

b

c

1 Start the grill for medium-high heat. Lay your chops out on your transport tray and blot them dry with a paper towel. Salt and pepper the meat on both sides (fig. a). Oil both sides of the pork chop to help conduct heat from the grill to the steak.

2 Place the pork on the hottest part of the grill (fig. b). Allow to cook for 2 minutes. If flames start to flare up from the bottom of the grill, give them a squirt of water from the bottle.

3 Rotate each chop 45 degrees on the same side to make a cross-hatch pattern. If it sticks to the grill as you're doing this, just wait another minute. As it browns it will stop sticking. Cook for another 2 minutes, then flip the pork chop and do the same thing on the other side (fig. c).

4 Insert a thermometer into a pork chop to check doneness. Make sure at least 1 full inch (2.5cm) of the thermometer stem is in the meat. When the temperature of 145°F (63°C) is reached, remove the pork chops from the grill onto a serving platter. Allow to rest for 5 minutes before eating.

 There are four basic steps to grilling foods: 1) Season and oil the food. 2) Put the food on the grill and allow it to cook halfway. 3) Turn over and cook the rest of the way. 4) Rest to allow juices to redistribute.

10

20 minutes

8 hours

INGREDIENTS

1 (8- to 10-lb. [3.5 to 4.5kg]) Boston pork roast

½ cup yellow mustard

1 cup barbeque rub

2 cups barbecue sauce (see recipe in Sauces and Condiments chapter)

TOOLS

Transport tray

Tongs

In-oven meat thermometer

Winter gloves

Extra-large rubber gloves

Serving platter

Slow cooker

Pulled Pork

Making pulled pork, which comes from the front shoulder of the pig, should be considered an art form unto itself. With every bite, you appreciate the layers of flavors, the spices, and the sauces.

1 Put the Boston roast skin side down on the transport tray, and dry with paper towels. Rub yellow mustard over every part of the pork (fig. a). Then rub all over with barbeque rub. Put the roast into the refrigerator to stay cool while you preheat the slow cooker to high.

2 Place the roast skin/fat side down in the cooker (fig. b). Cover and cook for 2 hours on high, then 6 hours on low.

3 Keep the lid closed until the end of the 8 hours. With a thermometer, check the pork roast for a reading of 182°F (89°C). If it's at least 182°F (89°C), remove from the cooker. Place the roast on a clean cutting board and allow to rest for 15 minutes.

4 Put on winter gloves and then extra-large rubber gloves over them. Follow the natural seams between muscles in the roast and separate them out, discarding connective tissue and fat (fig. c). Shred muscles to make pulled pork, keeping the delicious browned exterior separate to ensure that each guest gets a portion. Add barbeque sauce as desired. Put pulled pork on a platter to serve.

a

b

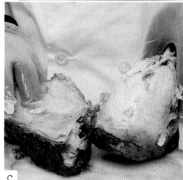
c

144   BEEF AND PORK

poultry

In this chapter, you'll learn about poultry and add two more cooking techniques to your repertoire. Frying is a technique that cooks things quickly and evenly in oil. And roasting is cooking savory foods in an oven. After learning the techniques and recipes in this chapter, you can begin to cook complex chicken, turkey, and duck dishes effectively.

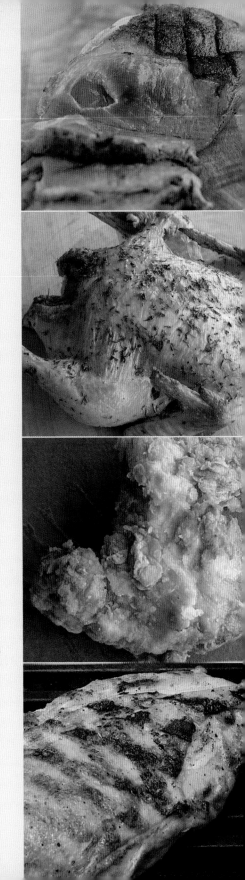

Poultry Basics

Poultry is widely available and less expensive than other meats, which makes it a very popular choice. Like other meats, the composition is high in water (72 percent) and low in fat (7 percent). The fat is not stored in the muscles like beef, but in the tail area, and it melts at lower temperatures. White meat and dark meat represent the tender and tougher cuts of meats. Tender white meat comes from muscles that don't get used much, while dark meat is from the muscles that do most of the work. Ducks don't have white meat because they have space to flap their wings. Chickens don't use their wings often, so their breast meat is white.

Buying

Poultry is available in most stores in a large variety of styles. You can get the meat whole, cut into pieces, marinated, and even as convenience foods that are hot and ready to eat. Poultry is easy to cut up, and a lot less expensive to buy whole, and if you buy it whole, you'll also have bones to use to make stock. I recommend you buy only whole, particularly chicken.

When you purchase poultry, you should check a couple of things for freshness. First, poultry shouldn't have a smell at all; if it has a rancid or ammonia smell, it's past its prime. You should also push on the flesh with one finger. If the flesh pops right back, that's a good sign it's fresh. If it leaves an indentation in the flesh, the meat is old and should be avoided. And don't be fooled into thinking a yellow skin color is the sign of a good-quality bird. The truth is, chickens can be fed specific things to alter the color of their skin. There is a USDA quality inspection system, but it's not required. If there is a grading stamp, look for grade "A."

Storing

Poultry is the most susceptible meat to cross-contamination and the growth of salmonella. Care should be taken to make sure nothing is stored under raw poultry in the refrigerator so the juices can't leak down onto other foods. As with any meat, poultry should be kept in a bowl so juices can't drip. Also, make sure the plastic it's wrapped in has holes in it so air can flow in, which will reduce the likelihood of the water in the flesh becoming rancid.

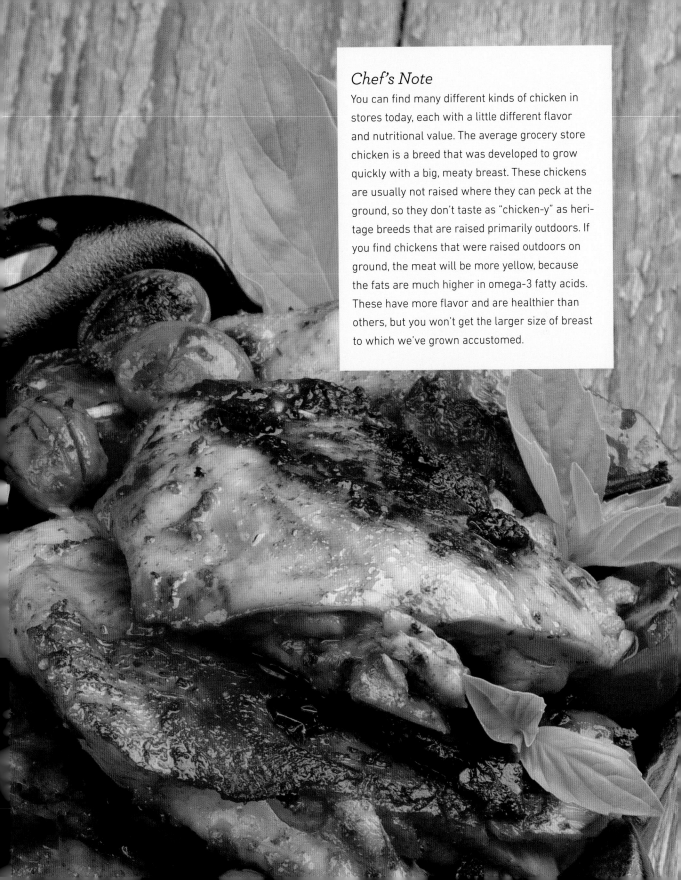

Chef's Note

You can find many different kinds of chicken in stores today, each with a little different flavor and nutritional value. The average grocery store chicken is a breed that was developed to grow quickly with a big, meaty breast. These chickens are usually not raised where they can peck at the ground, so they don't taste as "chicken-y" as heritage breeds that are raised primarily outdoors. If you find chickens that were raised outdoors on ground, the meat will be more yellow, because the fats are much higher in omega-3 fatty acids. These have more flavor and are healthier than others, but you won't get the larger size of breast to which we've grown accustomed.

How to Cut Up a Whole Chicken

INGREDIENTS

1 whole chicken

TOOLS

Sharp chef's knife
Cutting board
Transport tray

 Once you have finished, you will have the basic eight-piece cuts of chicken. Freeze the chicken pieces, and make stock with the body frame.

Once you've learned the ease of cutting a whole chicken into pieces, you'll never go back to buying pre-cut chicken. You'll have the leftover bones to make stock—a foundation for so many sauces and soups—and a whole chicken costs significantly less per pound.

1 Place chicken on a cutting board back side down, with the neck pointing toward you. Using a sharp chef's knife, slice down the top-middle of the breast until you reach the bone (fig. a). Follow the bone down and to the side, cutting under the breast meat. Follow the wishbone to where the wing attaches to the body.

2 Cut through the cartilage of the wing-body joint, and cut the skin between the thigh and the breast to free the breast (fig. b). Put the breast aside and repeat the process on the other side.

3 Turn the chicken around so the leg is pointing toward you. Near the base of the thigh, you should feel the hip joint (fig. c). Cut behind that thigh meat and in front of the hip bone to expose the joint.

4 Follow the outside of the body cavity around to the thigh-body joint. Cut through that joint to release the dark meat from the body (fig. d). Put the dark meat aside and repeat the process for the other side.

5 Move the thigh-leg quarters to the cutting board. Find the thin line of fat right above the joint, and cut straight down through it (fig. e). Your knife should come down cleanly between the bones. Repeat this for the other thigh-leg quarter. Move these finished pieces aside.

6 Move the breast quarters back to the cutting board, skin side up, and cut around the breast where the wing joint is attached (fig. f). Repeat this process with the other breast-wing quarter.

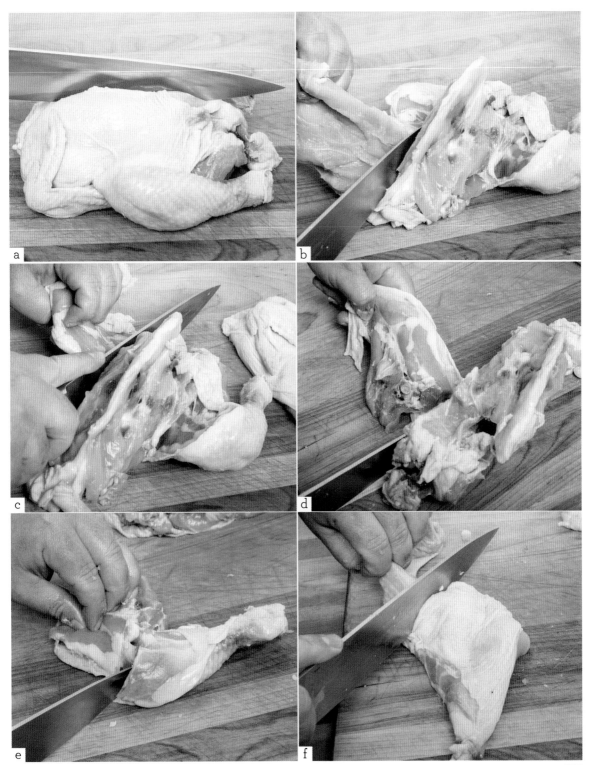

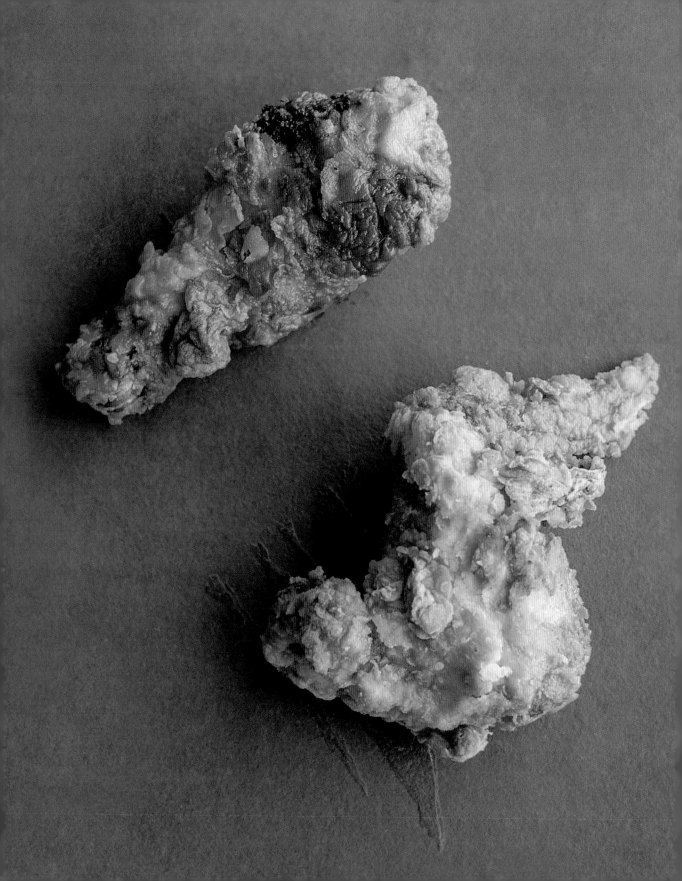

Fried Chicken

Frying is a dry-heat cooking method best suited for quick cooking tender cuts of meat or poultry. In this recipe the chicken is coated, allowed to rest, cooked, and seasoned to finish. These steps can be used for any tender cut of meat.

 4

 30 minutes

⏱ 20 minutes

INGREDIENTS

4-lb. (2kg) chicken, cut into 8 pieces

1 TB. kosher salt

1 tsp. black pepper

1 cup all-purpose flour

2 eggs

4 oz. (120mL) milk

3 cups peanut oil

TOOLS

Cast iron skillet

2 mixing bowls

High-temperature thermometer

Tongs

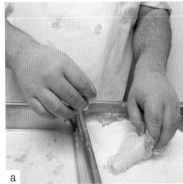

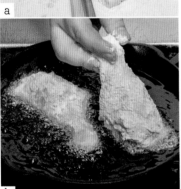

1 Season all parts of the chicken with salt and pepper. Put the flour into one bowl. In the other bowl, mix the eggs and milk.

2 Using one hand, dip the chicken in the flour, then the egg mixture (called *egg wash*), then back in the flour (fig. a). Place in a sheet pan until ready to fry. Do this with each piece of chicken, keeping one hand clean to do other things.

3 Heat the peanut oil in the skillet over high heat. You should have 1½ to 2 inches (4 to 5 cm) of oil. When the thermometer reaches 400°F (205°C), place the chicken into the oil carefully (fig. b).

4 Maintaining the oil at a temperature of 350°F (177°C), cook one side until it's Golden Brown and looks Delicious (GBD) (fig. c). Then turn and cook the other side.

5 Check the internal temperature of each piece of meat to make sure it's 160°F (71°C). If not, return it to the oil until finished. The pieces will cook at different rates.

 Chef's Tip
The resting time between coating and frying the chicken gives the flour, egg, and milk batter time to adhere to the chicken. If you fry the chicken immediately after coating it, the crust will fall off in clumps.

4

 30 minutes

 5 minutes

INGREDIENTS

4 (6-oz. [110g]) chicken breasts, boneless, skin on

1 TB. kosher salt

1 tsp. black pepper

¼ cup vegetable oil

TOOLS

Transport tray

Tongs

Squirt bottle of water

Meat thermometer

Grilled Chicken Breasts

Chicken is a blank canvas, and it's easy to create your own masterpieces. This recipe can be used to make a grilled chicken salad, or served with different sauces such as salsa, pesto, or barbeque. Each sauce gives the chicken a unique flavor profile.

1 Light the grill and preheat to medium heat. Season the chicken breasts on both sides with salt and pepper (fig. a). Coat both sides with oil (fig. b).

2 Place the chicken on the hottest part of the grill skin side down (fig. c). Allow to sit for 1 minute. If flames start to flare up from the bottom of the grill, give them a squirt of water.

3 Pick up each breast with tongs and rotate 45 degrees on the same side to make a cross-hatch pattern. If a breast sticks to the grill as you do this, wait another minute. As it browns the breast will stop sticking.

4 After another minute of cooking, flip each piece of chicken and do the same thing on the other side (fig. d).

5 Insert a thermometer into each breast to check for doneness. When a temperature of 160°F (71°C) is reached, remove the breasts from the grill onto a serving platter. Allow to rest for 5 minutes before eating.

Serve garnished with the sauce of your choice.

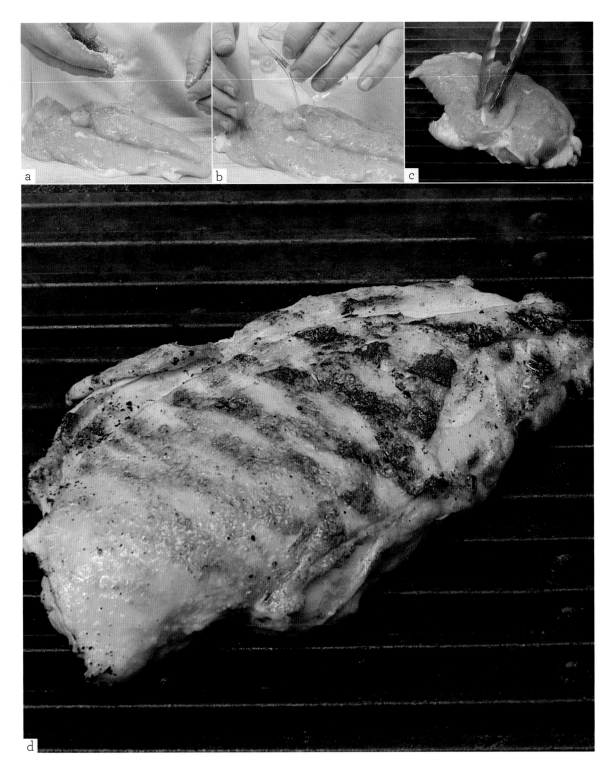

GRILLED CHICKEN BREASTS 155

Chef's Tip

Roasting can be broken down into four simple steps: season, cook, rest, and serve. The hard part is getting everything balanced. You have to use the right amount of seasoning to not overpower the flavor of the chicken. You need the right amount of dry heat to crisp the skin, but not so much the skin burns before the inside is done. And you have to let the chicken rest long enough for the juices to redistribute evenly, but not let the chicken get cold. Patience is the key.

Roasted Whole Chicken

The basic roasted chicken created in this recipe is one thing I think all good cooks should be able to do well. It's so simple in concept, but it's not so easy to achieve the perfect result.

 4

 10 minutes

 1 hour

INGREDIENTS

1 (5–6 lb. [2.3–2.7kg]) whole chicken

1 tsp. dried thyme leaves

1 tsp. rubbed sage

1 TB. kosher salt

1 tsp. white pepper

TOOLS

Sheet pan

Cooling rack

2 pairs of tongs

In-oven meat thermometer

Sharp chef's knife

Serving platter

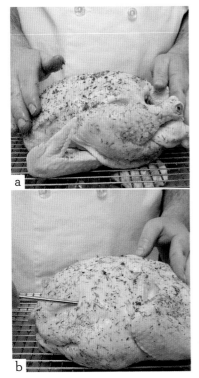

a

b

1 Remove the giblets and neck from the body cavity and place in a sheet pan. Dry the chicken with paper towels. Rub the seasonings on all parts of the bird—even inside the cavity (fig. a). Place a cooling rack on top of a sheet pan, and put the chicken breast down on the cooling rack. (You may have to place balled-up aluminum foil under the rack to keep the chicken straight.)

2 Place an in-oven thermometer in the thickest part of the thigh meat and cook at 350°F (177°C) for 15 minutes (fig. b). Then turn the chicken over and finish cooking with the breast side up. Don't open the oven again until the thermometer reaches 155°F (68°C).

3 When it reaches 155°F (68°C), remove the chicken from the oven. Allow it to rest in the pan for 15 minutes. During this time more juices may come out.

4 You can use the pan drippings to make the velouté variation in the Sauces and Condiments chapter. Cut into 8 pieces as instructed in "How to Cut Up a Whole Chicken".

18

 10 minutes

3 hours

Roasted Turkey

Nothing is more pleasant than the smell of turkey roasting in the oven during the holidays. Many people only eat roasted turkey for holiday dinners. But it's nutritious, inexpensive, and easy to cook—although it does have a long cooking time.

INGREDIENTS

1 (18-20 lb. [8-9kg])
  whole turkey

½ cup butter

1 TB. dried thyme leaves

1 TB. rubbed sage

3 TB. kosher salt

1 TB. white pepper

¼ tsp. nutmeg

TOOLS

Turkey roasting pan with
  rack

2 pairs of tongs

In-oven meat
  thermometer

Chef's knife

Serving platter

1 Make a compound butter by mixing the whole butter with all the seasonings (fig. a).

2 Remove the giblets and neck from the body cavity. Put them in the roasting pan. Dry the turkey with paper towels. Pull the skin away from the meat. Rub the seasoned butter into all parts of the bird under the skin (fig. b).

3 Place the turkey breast down on the rack. Insert an in-oven probe thermometer in the thickest part of the thigh meat (fig. c). Cook at a temperature of 250°F (121°C). Cook for 2 hours, turn the turkey over, and finish cooking with the breast side up.

4 Remove the turkey from the oven when the thermometer reaches 155°F (68°C). Allow it to rest for 20 minutes.

5 Cut the breasts off the bone, slicing across the grain of the meat. Put the breasts on a serving platter. Next remove the thighs and legs. Cut the meat off the thighs and put on the serving platter, along with the whole legs.

 Thawing a Turkey from Frozen

It takes five days for a frozen turkey to thaw in the refrigerator. I pull mine out of the freezer a week before I'm going to roast it so it has time to completely thaw. If you forget, clean your sink out and put the stopper in the drain. Put the turkey in and allow cold water to run gently into the sink. The flowing water will slowly warm up the turkey, but use only cold water. This process will still take at least four hours, and more likely eight.

a

b

c

Chef's Note

The turkey was first bred in Mexico more than 2,000 years ago. Shortly after that, another breed was developed in the American Southwest. It's still common to see turkey dishes in these areas gracing menus year-round.

How Long Does It Take to Cook a Turkey?

There are a lot of figures floating around about how many minutes it will take to cook a turkey, based on its weight. This number largely depends on how the turkey was raised and its water content. *The main thing to remember is you're cooking to a temperature, not to a time.* I cannot emphasize this enough. If the turkey goes over 165°F (71°C) on the inside, it will get dry as a desert. You always want to pull the turkey out of the oven when it reaches 155°F (68°C) so it can carryover cook to 165°F (71°C). I use a figure of cooking 18 minutes per pound as my starting point, then pull it and let it rest when it hits 155°F (68°C), no matter how long it has been in the oven.

10

 10 minutes

 Finished

INGREDIENTS

10-lb. (4.5kg) roast turkey

TOOLS

Cutting board

Chef knife

Long offset spatula

Serving platter

Carving a Roasted Turkey

Carrying a large whole turkey on a platter to the dining table to carve is probably the hardest way to serve it. It's much easier and cleaner to debone and carve the turkey in the kitchen, and arrange the slices on the platter.

1 Allow the roast turkey to rest for 20 minutes, and place it on the cutting board with the open cavity facing away from you. Place the knife at the top of the breast and draw it down along the rib cage (fig. a), keeping it against the ribs. You'll come to the joint where the wing attaches to the breast. Cut through the joint. If you're against the bone, readjust the knife to cut through the joint. The breast with attached wing should come free of the turkey. Set aside for slicing.

2 On the same side that you removed the breast, pull the thigh and leg down to see the joint where the thigh attaches to the body. Cut through the joint to remove the thigh and leg (fig. b). Lay the piece on the cutting board with the thigh skin down. Remove the leg from the thigh by cutting through the joint where they come together. Set aside.

3 Return to the breast that's still attached to the body. Remove the breast as in step 1 (fig. c).

4 Remove the second leg and thigh as in step 2 (fig. d). Remove the main body from the cutting board. This can be boiled to make stock for gravy.

5 Place the breasts back on the cutting board. Following the wing to where it meets the breast, cut straight down to remove the wing (fig. e). The wing can also be used for stock. Slice the breast and place each slice so the breast still looks whole. Slide a spatula under the sliced breast and move it to the serving platter. Repeat the process with the second breast.

6 Move the thighs to the cutting board. There's one bone in the thigh, and you can remove it by running your index finger between the bone and meat. Slice and move the thigh meat to the platter at the tapered end of the breasts. Repeat on the second thigh. Finish the platter by arranging the legs on the sides of the breasts (fig. f).

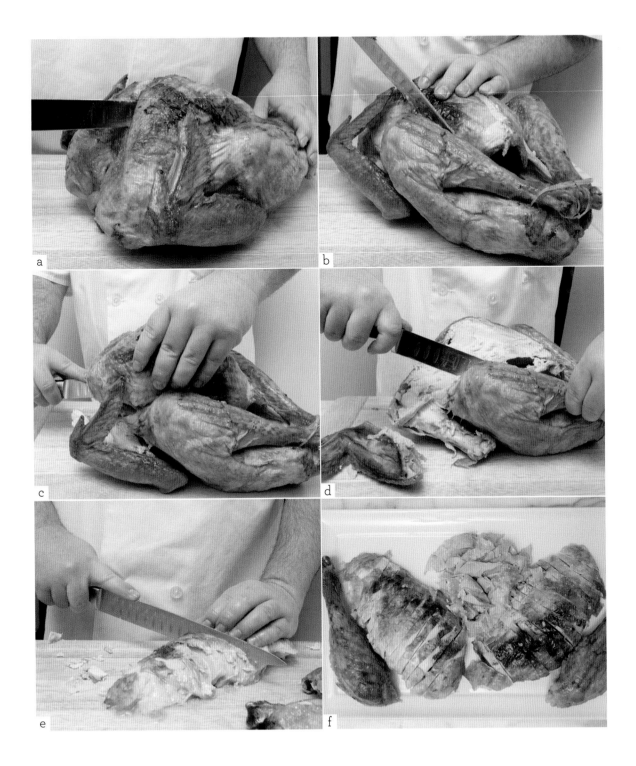

Chef's Note

There are three main breeds of domesticated ducks. The most common is the Pekin, the familiar white duck, which is known for mild flavor and long breasts, and is a descendant of the Mallard. Muscovy is a smaller bird with darker, gamier flavor, and is an entirely different genus. Then there's the Moulard (not to be confused with Mallard). It's a genetic cross between the Pekin and Muscovy birds and is the preferred bird for the dish foie gras.

Sautéed Duck Breasts

Duck takes on the characteristics of a sauce very well and is more nutritious than other commercial meats. The great thing about duck is the fat is just under the skin, so if it's cooked properly, it should come out lean.

 6

 10 minutes

12 minutes

INGREDIENTS

4 duck breasts, skin on

3 TB. kosher salt

1 TB. black pepper

TOOLS

Iron skillet

Pair of tongs

Instant-read thermometer

Sharp slicing knife

Serving platter

a

b

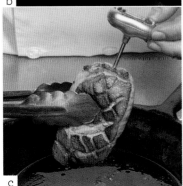

c

1   Dry the duck with paper towels. Slice through the skin just to the meat on a diagonal every ½ inch (1.25cm) (fig. a). Salt and pepper both sides of the breasts. Do not oil the exterior as you do other sauté items.

2   Place the frying pan on high heat. When it's hot, add the meat skin side down (fig. b). Allow to cook until the skin is GBD (Golden Brown and looks Delicious).

3   Turn the duck over and insert a thermometer in the thickest part of the breast (fig. c). Once the internal temperature has risen to 155°F (68°C), remove to a cutting board.

4   Allow the breasts to rest for 15 minutes. Slice the duck at a 45-degree angle ("on the bias") to make the muscle strands shorter and tenderer. You should get 1½ servings from each breast.

 How to Make Duck Taste Less Greasy

In this recipe you cut through the skin of the duck, but not into the meat. Ducks store their fat between the skin and meat, and it keeps them warm during cold weather. Cutting into the skin gives the oil a path out as it's warmed, which produces a leaner duck.

seafood

In this chapter, you'll learn the fundamentals of cooking fish and other seafood. The recipes will teach you the essential skills of pan frying, broiling, marinating, searing, and more. In addition, you'll learn how to buy the freshest fish and seafood and how to store it properly.

Fish Basics

Fish is a great source of protein that, for the most part, is leaner than other meats. Many health-conscious people also look to fish for healthy fats, minerals, and vitamins that are harder to get from other single sources of food. The demand for good fish has increased as more people have learned about these benefits.

Buying

Fish aren't normally graded the way other meats are. For a fee, fish and seafood companies can voluntarily have their facilities and fish inspected, but few ever do. This makes it very important that you check the quality of the fish before you purchase. If it's a whole fish, make sure the eyes are clear, not cloudy. And the gills should be red; if they're brown, don't buy the fish. For whole fish or individual filets, press down on the meat; if the flesh springs back and doesn't leave an indentation, it's fresh. Finally, smell the fish. If it has a sweet smell, it's fresh. If it has a bad or strong fishy odor, don't buy it.

Storing

Fish has only a few days' shelf life if it's handled correctly. Because of this, you should go to great lengths to take care of your treasure. It's best to store it with ice directly on top of the fish using a roasting pan and a rack. Place the fish on top of the rack, cover it with ice, and keep it in the refrigerator covered with plastic wrap. As the ice melts, the water should be able to run off without the fish lying in it. For the best quality, use within two days.

 Chef's Note

Due to the increase in consumption of seafood, there's concern that some species of fish may become extinct due to overfishing. Several programs have been established to monitor the populations of fish, as well as the methods used to farm-raise fish. These programs put together lists showing which fish are better to eat based on the fishing and farming methods used. The Monterey Bay Aquarium at montereybayaquarium.org is a good place to find lists you can print and take with you to the market when you purchase fish.

Chef's Tip

Most salmon you find in stores is farm-raised Atlantic salmon kept in pens in the middle of the ocean. A couple of concerns have been raised regarding this method. Chemicals are added to the waters to control the populations of worms that burrow into the salmon's flesh, and these chemicals can drift into open waters, as well. Another concern is that Atlantic salmon are being raised in pens located in the Pacific Ocean. Often fish escape into the wild, and there's concern that they'll become an invasive species in the Pacific. It's recommended that you check seafood monitoring authorities such as the Monterey Bay Aquarium to learn what fish are safe before you buy.

4

 10 minutes

 10 minutes

INGREDIENTS

4 (6-oz. [170g]) salmon
  filets, skin on
1 TB. sea salt
1 tsp. white pepper
2 TB. vegetable oil

TOOLS

Heavy-bottomed sauté
  pan
Offset spatula or tongs

Sautéed Salmon

Fish flesh has a very delicate structure, so it's important to handle it with great care. When cooking, never pick up the fish from the flesh side as you are likely to penetrate the meat.

1 Season the filets with salt and pepper on both sides (fig. a). With seafood, it's best to use sea salt to accent the flavors. Use white pepper so you don't get the flecks black pepper would leave. Rub the oil on all sides of the fish after it's seasoned.

2 Preheat the sauté pan over high heat. When the pan is blazing hot, place the fish skin side down (fig. b). Don't overcrowd the pan. Cook the fish on the skin side for 5 minutes to form a crispy skin. Then turn and cook the flesh side for 3 minutes (fig. c).

3 Remove the filets from the pan onto serving plates. The fish should rest for 2 minutes before you eat so its juices are evenly distributed.

a

b

c

 Chef's Tip
Salmon pairs well with pesto sauce or one of the sauces based on velouté.

SEAFOOD

SEAFOOD

Pan-Fried Tilapia

Tilapia is a mild white fish that has become increasingly popular in many areas in recent years. It's a thin fish, so the filets are perfect for pan frying.

 4

 10 minutes

 4 minutes

INGREDIENTS

4 (4-6 oz. [110-170g]) tilapia filets

1 TB. sea salt

1 tsp. white pepper

½ cup flour

4 cups vegetable oil (amount will vary with size of skillet used)

TOOLS

Cast iron skillet

1-qt. (1L) pot

High-temperature thermometer

2-oz. (60mL) metal ladle

Sheet pan lined with paper towels

Offset spatula

1 Pour 2 cups of oil in the skillet and 2 cups in the 1-quart pot. Heat the oil in both the skillet and the pot to 350°-375°F (177°-190°C) measured with a high-temperature thermometer. Adjust the flame to keep the oil temperature in that range.

2 Season the fish with salt and pepper (fig. a) and roll in flour (fig b.). Carefully put the fish into the hot oil in the skillet (fig. c). If the oil is more than halfway up the side of the fish, ladle a little out into the other pot. If it's less than halfway, add oil from the pot to get to the halfway point. Cook for 2 minutes on one side.

3 Using an offset spatula, turn the fish and cook an additional 2 minutes (fig. d). (Always turn it away from you so the hot oil doesn't splash on you.)

4 Remove the fish from the skillet onto a sheet pan lined with paper towels.

Serve with one of the variations of mayonnaise found in the Sauces and Condiments chapter.

 Essential Technique: Pan Frying

Pan frying is similar to sautéing and deep frying in that the food is cooked using oil as a medium to transfer the heat. When pan frying, the oil should be halfway up the side of the food being cooked. If it's more than halfway, you might burn a ring around the side of the food. If it's less than halfway, the food may not cook in the middle. The basic process of pan frying is simple: season the food, coat it with flour, and cook. The trick is to keep some hot oil on the side to adjust the level as needed.

4

 10 minutes

 8 minutes

INGREDIENTS

8 trout filets

1 TB. sea salt

1 tsp. white pepper

1 TB. lime juice

2 cups unseasoned
 breadcrumbs

1 clove garlic, minced

1 TB. lemon juice

2 TB. melted whole butter

TOOLS

Small mixing bowl

Sheet pan

Offset spatula

Broiled Trout

Broiling is a cooking technique in which the heat comes from above the food. This is a good process for cooking thin items that benefit from browning. In this recipe, we're using a very thin fish filet and browning bread-crumbs on top for a richer flavor.

1 Move a rack to the highest shelf in the oven. Preheat the broiler. Cut through the skin of the trout in five different places, but don't cut into the flesh (fig. a). This will help keep it from curling when it's cooked.

2 Season both sides of the fish with salt and pepper and sprinkle with lime juice (fig. b). Place the fish on a sheet pan so the skin side is up.

3 In the bowl, combine breadcrumbs, garlic, lemon juice, and butter (fig. c).

4 Place the trout under the broiler for 4 minutes.

5 Remove the fish from the broiler. Turn with the offset spatula (fig. d). Put a layer of breadcrumbs on each piece. Return to the oven for about 2 minutes, until the breadcrumbs are toasted but not burned.

 Chef's Tip

Nutty grains such as couscous pair well with this trout as the flavors will enhance the toasted quality of the breadcrumbs. Serving it with grilled summer squash will create a lighter feel to the entrée and provide a fresh flavor.

🍴 *Chef's Tip*

Many restaurants serve a lemon wedge with fish to balance the flavors. Instead, I recommend pairing a nice glass of white wine with an acid backbone instead. A bright glass of Sauvignon Blanc would work much better than a lemon.

Shellfish Basics

The shellfish classification includes a vast array of mostly aquatic creatures. Shellfish include crustaceans such as lobsters, crabs, and shrimp, and bivalves such as oysters, mussels, and clams. There are a few common ground rules to follow when buying and storing these treasures.

Buying

When you buy live bivalve shellfish, you want to make sure the shells are closed tightly. If bivalve shells are open, that's a sign that they're dead and should not be eaten. If they're crustaceans, they should be moving their legs. Next, smell the shellfish. They should have a sweet smell like the ocean at high tide. If they have a bad smell, steer clear of them and anything around them. Especially bad is the smell of ammonia, which is a sign that they're decaying.

Shellfish is often sold frozen because it's the best way to transport the product and maintain its freshness. There are a couple of things to look for when buying frozen shellfish. Don't purchase it if there are any ice crystals, which is a sign it has been thawed and re-frozen. Avoid the shellfish if the box is torn or crushed in any way.

When buying scallops and shrimp, the number listed for sizing refers to how many of each it will take to add up to a pound. Thus, with 28-32 size shrimp there will be 28 to 32 in a pound. They're often sold in 3-pound boxes. Multiply the size number by the box size and you'll come up with the number of pieces in the box. The largest of the sizes is normally U-10 (for Under 10), which would mean there are fewer than 10 items in a pound.

Storing

Shellfish should be stored at a temperature near freezing. The best way to maintain this temperature is to put ice in a bag and place it on top of the crustaceans in the refrigerator. Never cover live crustaceans with plastic wrap, which will cause them to suffocate and make them no longer safe to eat. Serve shellfish within two days of purchasing.

If the seafood was purchased frozen, it's best to thaw it in the refrigerator. If it's needed quickly, put the frozen shellfish into a plastic bag and thaw under cold running water.

Shrimp Cocktail

Many people consider shrimp cocktail an elegant and iconic dish. It's a classic because it tastes so good, yet is so simple to make. Don't buy the pre-cooked shrimp for this dish; cooking raw shrimp in a savory liquid will bring out richer flavors.

 4

 20 minutes

 30 minutes

INGREDIENTS

2 qt. (2L) water

2 bay leaves

4 TB. kosher salt

5 juniper berries, whole

10 peppercorns, whole

2 oranges, cut in half

24 shrimp, 10-16 size, peeled and deveined, tail on, raw

1 cup cocktail sauce (see recipe in the Sauces and Condiments chapter)

TOOLS

1-gallon pot

Colander

1 Combine water and spices in a pot. Bring up to a boil over high heat (fig. a). After it has come to a boil, squeeze the oranges into the water and throw in the whole orange, as well.

2 Add the shrimp to the boiling water, and immediately turn off the flame (fig. b).

3 After 4 minutes, strain the shrimp out of the water through a colander (fig. c). Put the shrimp on a sheet pan and place in the refrigerator to cool for 20 minutes.

4 After the shrimp have cooled, arrange them on plates and serve to your guests with your homemade cocktail sauce.

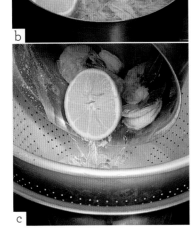

4

 20 minutes

 4 minutes

INGREDIENTS

2 TB. orange juice

2 TB. lemon juice

1 TB. soy sauce

1 TB. sesame oil

1 clove garlic, minced

1 tsp. ginger powder

2 tsp. sea salt

1 tsp. white pepper

24 shrimp, U-10 size,
   peeled and deveined, tail
   on, raw

2 TB. vegetable oil

TOOLS

2 medium mixing bowls

Whisk

Tongs

Grill

Serving platter

Grilled Shrimp

Marinating is a way of adding extra flavors to foods before they're cooked. The marinade used in this recipe has both an acid and a salt component, which gives the grilled shrimp a juicier finish.

1 Light the grill and allow it to come up to a hot temperature. In a bowl, whisk together all the ingredients except the vegetable oil. Place the shrimp in the marinade and allow to marinate for 15 minutes (fig. a).

2 Drain the marinade off the shrimp, and coat with vegetable oil (fig. b).

3 Place the shrimp on the hot grill (fig. c). Grill 2 minutes on one side of the shrimp, turn them over, and cook an additional 2 minutes (fig. d).

Serve the shrimp while they're still hot. This pairs well with a salsa with pineapple added.

 Chef's Tip

The acid in a marinade will remove liquids and toughen the meat if it marinates too long. For seafood, you only need to marinate for 15 minutes before cooking. For poultry, 2 hours is the maximum time. Other meats can marinate up to 24 hours without any problems.

Crab Cakes

This recipe features the rich flavor of crab. When you purchase whole crabs, a lot of parts get thrown out, so for this recipe it's best to buy cans of picked crab meat, which often are found in the butcher's case.

 4

 20 minutes, 1 hour to rest

 6 minutes

a

b

c

1 Combine all ingredients except the crab and pan spray. Mix to combine well, but not so much that it becomes a soggy mess (fig. a). Pick through the crab to check for pieces of shell.

2 Make the mixture into patties (fig. b). Lay them out on the sheet pan, and spray with pan release spray on both sides. Put them in the refrigerator for a minimum of 1 hour.

3 Preheat the oven to 400°F (205°C). Put the skillet on high heat. When the pan is very hot, sauté the crab cakes for 2 minutes and carefully turn to the other side (fig. c). As soon as you turn them, place them in the oven for 4 minutes.

4 Remove from the oven and arrange on a platter. Garnish with salsa. These crab cakes are also fantastic with arugula greens as a salad.

INGREDIENTS

2 limes, zest only

1 green onion, white and green parts, chopped

3 oz. (85g) cooked bacon, chopped

½ cup mayonnaise

1 large egg

½ cup bread crumbs

2 tsp. Old Bay seasoning

1½ tsp. sea salt

1½ lbs. lump crab meat

Pan release spray

1 cup cocktail sauce (see the recipe in the Sauces and Condiments chapter)

TOOLS

Mixing bowl

Sheet pan

Cast iron skillet

Offset spatula

Serving platter

4

 2 hours

 6 minutes

INGREDIENTS

16 oysters, fresh

1 cup whole butter, left
out to soften for 2 hours

4 cloves garlic, minced

1 tsp. tarragon, chopped

¼ tsp. thyme leaves

TOOLS

Oyster knife

Kitchen towel

Sheet pan

Pair of tongs

Serving platter

Transport tray

Grilled Oysters

Oysters are wonderful, as long as you buy them when they're really fresh. They have a delicately sweet and briny balance. This recipe heats shelled oysters directly over the grill to melt in the accompanying herb butter.

 How to Shuck an Oyster

1. An oyster has two shells, one flat and the other more rounded (fig. a). You want to leave the rounded side down so the liquid stays in as you open the oyster.

2. Roll up a kitchen towel, leaving a flap of 2 inches (5cm). Place the rounded end of the oyster in the towel where the roll meets the flap. This leaves the part of the oyster with the hinge sticking out the back.

3. Put one hand behind the roll to hold the oyster (fig. b). That way if the knife slips out of the oyster, the blade should go into the towel (and not your hand).

4. With the oyster knife in the other hand, put the point between the oyster's hinge and pry it open (fig. c).

5. Run the knife around the inside of the oyster to free the meat from the shell. Repeat on the bottom shell, but leave as much juice as you can. Discard the top shells. Line up the bottom shells containing meat on a transport tray.

1 Preheat the grill on medium high.

2 Combine the butter, garlic, and herbs to make an herb-compound butter. Put a tablespoon of garlic herb butter on each shucked oyster.

3 Place the oysters on the hottest part of the grill (fig. d). You have to keep them balanced upright. After 6 minutes, the butter should be melted. Remove the oysters to the serving platter.

The shells will stay warm for a long period of time. Oysters and champagne are a great way to start a dinner party.

SEAFOOD

a

b

c

d

SEAFOOD

Seared Scallops

Searing is similar to sautéing, except an item being seared stays on the heat longer to give it a thicker outer crust. The steps in this recipe can be used on most tender cuts of meat $1/2$ to 1 inch (1.25 to 2.5cm) thick.

 4

 2 minutes

 3 minutes

INGREDIENTS

2 lb. (1kg) scallops, U-10 size, dry packed, side muscle removed

$1/2$ TB. sea salt

$1/2$ tsp. white pepper

$1/2$ cup vegetable oil

TOOLS

Cast iron skillet

Tongs

Offset spatula

Serving bowl

1 Season the scallops with salt and pepper (fig. a), then toss with the vegetable oil (fig. b). Preheat the skillet to the smoking point and put in the scallops.

2 Sear for 3 minutes. You should see the sides of the bottom of the scallop start to brown (fig. c). When the browning is about ¼ inch (6.35mm) up the side, turn and sear the other side for 3 minutes (fig. d).

3 Remove the scallops from the skillet. These are fabulous served with a béchamel-based cream sauce.

Wet Pack versus Dry Pack
When scallops or other seafood are wet packed, a chemical is added to make them last longer. Unfortunately, this chemical also retards the browning process during cooking, so it's hard to sauté or sear wet-packed seafood. Dry-packed seafood isn't chemically treated, so searing is much easier. Don't be fooled when you buy scallops. A wet pack will have less liquid in the container than a dry pack. The wet pack chemical causes the scallops to soak up the liquid, which increases the cost if you pay by the pound.

Smoke Warning
Searing, as well as sautéing, tends to produce a lot of smoke. Be sure to turn on the fan over the stove; otherwise, you may set off a fire alarm.

pastas and grains

In this chapter, you'll learn the fundamentals of cooking with pasta and grains, such as rice and quinoa. The recipes will teach you the essential skills of working with dried pastas and grains. In addition, you'll learn the versatility of starches and how to pair sauces with different types of pasta.

Pasta Basics

Pasta is a staple in homes throughout the world. It has been claimed that Marco Polo first brought pasta to Italy from China, but Europeans were actually eating various pastas long before his trips. In fact, pasta has been a staple food for people around the world for thousands of years.

Buying Pasta

Pasta is simply flour that has been mixed with a liquid, usually water or eggs. Once the dough is made, it can be formed into literally thousands of shapes with melodic and poetic names such as *spaghettini*, *fusilli, orecchiette,* and *tagliatelle*. In today's grocery stores, you can find dozens of these varieties in dried forms. The better quality manufacturers use semolina flour, a more flavorful hard flour. High-quality dried pasta should be a yellow color, not greyish-white. If the maker uses copper equipment, the pasta will come out looking like it's dusted with flour, and this is a good thing, because it helps the sauce stick to the finished pasta.

After you've purchased the perfect dried pasta, you want to make sure it's stored correctly, so keep it in an airtight container away from moisture and it will be good for years.

Cooking Pasta

Picking the right pasta for the right sauce is the first step. Long strands, such as spaghetti, linguini, and angel hair, are better for oil and thicker sauces. With thinner sauces and meat sauces, tubular pastas that have nooks and crannies, such as rigatoni and penne, work better, because the thin sauces will stick in the tubes and the meats will get stuck in the nooks and crannies.

After you've chosen the right pasta for the dish, you'll need to decide how much to cook. As a general rule, 1 pound (450g) of dried pasta will swell to 3 pounds (1.5kg) once cooked. This is enough for four to six people when enjoyed as an entrée.

6

 15 minutes

about 12 minutes
(varies by shape)

INGREDIENTS

1 gal. water

4 TB. salt

1 lb. (450g) dried pasta

TOOLS

Large pot

Metal spoon

Strainer

Pasta bowl

Cooking Dried Pasta

This is the standard way of cooking dried pasta that has been repeated thousands of times per day. Bring a gallon of salted water to a boil, add one pound of dried pasta, wait until it's cooked, and drain.

1 Combine water and salt in a pot. Bring to a boil.

2 Add dried pasta to the pot (fig. a). Give it a light stir every 2 minutes. When the pasta starts to feel soft, taste it. If it's still firm but no longer has a crunch, strain immediately (fig. b). A matter of 1 minute extra could allow the pasta to overcook and become mushy.

3 Immediately after it's strained, toss the pasta with a little bit of the sauce it will be served with (fig. c). This helps keep it from sticking together, and the sauce will be absorbed into the pasta.

a

b

c

Cooking Dried Pasta: Facts and Myths

While this cooking method has been the standard for centuries, many cooks have variations, and some disagree on a couple of points:

Add salt, or no salt in the water? Most dried pasta doesn't have salt added. The salt in the water helps deliver the flavor better in the finished product. If you're using pasta that's already salted, you won't need to add salt to the water.

Add oil to the water? My mom always added olive oil to keep the pot from boiling over and making a mess. It did keep bubbles down in the pot, but when it was strained, the oil stayed on the pasta and kept the sauce from sticking. Don't add oil to the water, just keep an eye on the pot so it doesn't boil over.

Start with boiling water or cold water? You can get the same results by putting pasta in a smaller pot, adding cold water, and then bringing it up to a boil. The pasta gets hydrated with the cold water and cooks as it comes up to the boil. You just need to give it a little stir every few minutes.

Chef's Tip

Want to bring the mac and cheese dish up to the adult level?
Add ½ pound (225g) of one or more of these items when you
pour the mixture into the pan:

Bacon (cooked and chopped)

Shrimp (raw and chopped)

Lobster (raw and chopped)

Lump crab

Pulled pork BBQ

Bleu cheese

Roasted vegetables

Macaroni and Cheese

Rich, creamy macaroni and cheese is a comfort food that takes most people back to their childhood. This recipe combines the cream sauce béchamel (see the Sauces and Condiments chapter) with cheddar to make a delicious cheesy sauce.

 6

 1¹/₂ hours

 30 minutes

INGREDIENTS

1 qt. (1L) béchamel sauce

1 tsp. dry mustard

1 tsp. kosher salt

1 tsp. hot chile sauce

1 lb. (450g) grated cheddar cheese

½ cup breadcrumbs

1 lb. (450g) dried elbow macaroni

Pan spray

TOOLS

1-gal. pot

2-qt. (2L) pot

Wooden spoon

Whisk

Baking dish

a

1 Preheat oven to 300°F (149°C). Combine béchamel, mustard, salt, hot sauce, and cheese in a 2-quart (1L) pot (fig. a). Whisk together to incorporate. Bring to a simmer, whisking every 3 to 4 minutes.

2 Boil the macaroni in a 1-gallon pot using the directions for cooking dried pasta. After straining, add macaroni back to the pot and mix with the cheese sauce (fig. b).

b

3 Pour into a baking dish that has been sprayed with pan spray. Smooth out the mixture. Sprinkle the breadcrumbs across the top (fig. c). Place in the oven to roast until the crumbs are a delicious golden brown, about 15 minutes.

4 Let the macaroni and cheese rest at room temperature for 20 minutes, then cut and serve.

c

Lasagna

 12

 10 minutes

 1 hour

INGREDIENTS

1 lb. (450g) bulk Italian sausage

1 yellow onion, diced

1 green pepper, diced

15 oz. (425g) ricotta cheese

28-oz. (794g) can diced tomatoes

8 oz. (240mL) tomato sauce

16-oz. (454g) box lasagna noodle sheets

8 oz. (227g) sharp ched-dar cheese, shredded

25 slices pepperoni sausage

8 oz. (227g) Monterey Jack cheese, shredded

8 oz. (227g) mozzarella cheese, shredded

8 oz. (227g) Parmesan cheese, grated

TOOLS

Large sauté pan

9 × 13-in. (23 × 33cm) pan

6-oz. (180mL) ladle

Wooden spoon

This recipe inspired me to enroll in culinary school. I made this lasagna and doubled the amount of sausage, causing the oil in the pan to overflow. When I opened the oven door, a fireball shot across the kitchen. This is a safer variation of the original Fireball Lasagna.

1 Preheat the oven to 350°F (177°C). In a large pan over medium-high heat, brown the sausage along with the onion and green pepper. Drain the excess oil. Add the ricotta cheese, diced tomatoes, and tomato sauce and turn off the flame. Mix well.

2 Place a small amount of the mixture in a 9 × 13-inch (23 × 33cm) pan. Put in a layer of raw noodles. Sprinkle on the cheddar. Spread half of the ricotta/tomato sauce evenly in the pan. Add the next layer of noodles. Sprinkle on the Monterey Jack. Layer on pepperoni and then another ⅓ of sauce. Add another layer of noodles and the remaining sauce and top with the mozzarella.

3 Cover the dish with plastic wrap and then aluminum foil. Place it in the 350°F (177°C) oven for 45 minutes.

4 Take out of the oven and remove the foil and plastic wrap. Sprinkle the Parme-san on top of the lasagna and return the dish to the oven. Turn the oven to broil and brown the cheese. Remove and allow the lasagna to rest for 20 minutes.

Pasta Salad

Pasta salad is a versatile side dish. It goes great with barbeque on a hot summer day, or as a side for a midday sandwich. This is a quick and easy recipe that can be stored in the refrigerator for up to a week after making.

 12

 10 minutes

 12 minutes

INGREDIENTS

1 lb. (450g) rotini pasta

6 oz. (180mL) mayonnaise

1 red pepper, medium diced

1 yellow pepper, medium diced

1 green pepper, medium diced

2 green onions, chopped

1 head leaf lettuce

TOOLS

1-gal. pot

Strainer

Wooden spoon

Serving platter

a

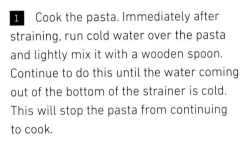

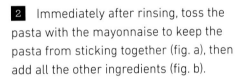
b

1 Cook the pasta. Immediately after straining, run cold water over the pasta and lightly mix it with a wooden spoon. Continue to do this until the water coming out of the bottom of the strainer is cold. This will stop the pasta from continuing to cook.

2 Immediately after rinsing, toss the pasta with the mayonnaise to keep the pasta from sticking together (fig. a), then add all the other ingredients (fig. b).

3 Put the lettuce leaves on the platter. Scoop the pasta salad on top of the lettuce leaves and serve (fig. c).

c

 Chef's Note

If pasta isn't going to be served hot right after it's cooked, it needs to be cooled quickly. Pasta continues to cook unless the temperature is brought down fast. In this recipe, the pasta is cooled under running water. You wouldn't want to do this if you'll be using thin sauces, as the water would wash away the starches that hold the sauces to the pasta.

6

 20 minutes

 18 minutes

INGREDIENTS

½ lb. (225g) Italian
  sausage

1 yellow onion

1 clove garlic

1 qt. (1L) tomato sauce

1 lb. (450g) pound
  spaghetti

TOOLS

Large sauté pan

1-gal. pot

Wooden spoon

Strainer

Serving bowl

Spaghetti and Meat Sauce

Spaghetti with meat sauce is an American-Italian dish that has become a staple for families of all ethnicities. The base this dish is built upon is the tomato sauce recipe in the Sauces and Condiments chapter. We sauté the added ingredients with the classic tomato sauce to create a savory sauce.

1 Break the sausage up into crumbles and sauté it in a hot sauté pan.

2 Once the sausage has browned, add the onions and sauté until translucent (fig. a). Turn off the flame and add the garlic. Mix the meat mixture.

3 Add the tomato sauce to the meat and bring to a simmer (fig. b). Let this simmer while the pasta is being cooked.

4 Cook the spaghetti until it's still firm but not crunchy, and strain when it's done (fig. c).

5 While it's still hot, add the pasta to the meat sauce and mix (fig. d).

 Variations on Sauce

Marinara: Don't add meat; just use the tomato sauce.

Fra Diavolo: Leave out the meat and add 1 tablespoon of crushed red pepper to the sauce.

Puttanesca: Instead of adding meat and sautéing, add ¼ cup of capers, ½ cup of green peppers, and ½ cup black of olives and sauté. Then add the tomato sauce.

SPAGHETTI AND MEAT SAUCE

Grains Basics

Grains are the edible seeds produced by grasses. The most popular of all grains include rice, corn, and wheat, and these three grains are essential components in the basic diets of most of the world's population.

Rice is common in most cultures, and is a staple food for more than half of the people in this world. Rice is categorized primarily into one of two types: *long-grain* and *short-grain*. The shorter the grain (and more round), the higher the starch content. So a long-grain rice should turn out fluffy after being cooked, while the higher starch content causes short-grained rice to be sticky.

Brown versus White Rice

Typically, all rice starts out as brown rice. This means the grain has both the endosperm and germ and only the husk has been removed, which makes brown rice higher in nutritional value. White rice has the germ removed as well, which makes the rice more stable so it lasts longer before oxidizing. White rice will cook in about half the time it takes brown rice to cook.

Converted rice is cooked before the germ and husk are removed. This pushes some of the nutrients from the exterior into the white part of the rice, so converted white rice is more nutrient dense that regular white rice, and it takes a few minutes longer to cook converted rice than plain white rice.

Wild rice is not in the same grass family as other rice, it actually comes from a reed rather than a grass. The seeds of wild rice are longer and a bit tougher than other rice, so it typically takes about three times longer to cook than plain white rice.

Purchasing and Storing Grains

When you purchase any type of grain, look for bright, clean seeds. They should not be dusty or smell musty.

Store grains in an airtight container in a cool place away from bright light; an airtight container will prevent moisture from hydrating the seeds. Storing in a cool area helps keep bugs away, and the low light level keeps grains from oxidizing and losing their nutrition. Whole grains should be refrigerated because the germ of the seed is high in fats, which can oxidize quickly if left in the open air.

 Quinoa Pilaf

Supergrains have been in existence since ancient times, and tend to have high levels of proteins and many other nutritional benefits. Quinoa is considered a supergrain and can generally be cooked exactly like rice. This rice pilaf recipe would also work well for quinoa—just replace the rice with quinoa.

Rice Pilaf

Pilaf might sound easy to cook, but in reality it can be difficult. If you take the lid off at the wrong time, it can be dry. If it's cooked too long, it can be mushy. But if you follow these steps, your rice will be fluffy and flavorful.

 8

 5 minutes

 22 minutes

INGREDIENTS

½ yellow onion, minced

2 TB. vegetable oil

1 cup basmati rice

2 cups chicken stock

1 tsp. kosher salt

TOOLS

1-qt. (1L) sauce pot

Lid for pot, or aluminum foil

Kitchen fork

Wooden spoon

1 Preheat the oven to 250°F (120°C). In the sauce pot, sweat the onion in vegetable oil over medium heat until it's translucent, but hasn't developed color (fig. a).

2 Add the rice and cook with the onion until it turns white and smells like popcorn (fig. b).

3 Add the stock and salt, and bring to a boil (fig. c).

4 The moment it comes to a boil, cover the pot and put it in the oven (fig. d). Cook for 20 minutes (do not open the oven during this time).

5 After 20 minutes, remove from the oven. Uncover and mix with the kitchen fork to fluff. Serve as a side dish.

6

 10 minutes

 22 minutes

INGREDIENTS

2 TB. butter

½ yellow onion, minced

1 cup arborio rice

2 cups chicken stock

½ cup dry white wine

½ cup heavy cream

2 tsp. kosher salt

1 oz. (25g) Parmesan
cheese, grated

TOOLS

Large straight-sided
sauté pan

Wooden spoon

Grater

Risotto

In this recipe we use a short-grain rice that contains much more starch, which makes the grains sticky when cooked. Mixing the risotto constantly while cooking breaks down the starch and adds a creamy texture to the finished dish.

1 In the sauté pan, sweat the onions in the butter over medium heat until they're translucent but have not developed color. Add the rice and mix until it's coated with the butter (fig. a).

2 Add 1 cup of stock and cook on medium-high heat until all the liquid has steamed away (fig. b). Be sure to continue to stir slowly the entire time. Repeat this process with the second cup of stock.

3 Add the wine, cream, cheese, and salt. Continue to stir again until the rice is cooked through (fig. c). The risotto should be very moist and creamy.

4 Draw your spoon through the risotto (fig. d). If you can make a line, the risotto has been cooked *au sec* (which translates to "almost dry"), and is ready to be served.

 Chef's Tip

There may be some variation when you cook this dish, depending on how hot the stove gets, the weight of the sauté pan, the moisture content of the air, and how hard you stir the rice. As with all foods, it's important that you taste and evaluate before serving. If the rice is still a bit crunchy, add a little more stock and cook it down again. If it lacks flavor, add salt and pepper.

Variations

To make different flavored risottos, simply add other ingredients with the wine and cream.

Lobster: add 8 ounces chopped lobster meat.

Mushroom: add ¼ cup mushroom duxelles.

Pesto: add ¼ cup prepared pesto.

Spinach: add 5 ounces of chopped spinach.

Couscous

Couscous is traditionally a hard cracked wheat berry that has been crushed in the milling process. This dish is often served with braised and stewed meats. It's also fantastic cold, tossed with some Italian-style salad dressing, peppers, and onions and served as a salad.

  4

 5 minutes

 5 minutes

INGREDIENTS

1½ cups chicken stock

1 tsp. kosher salt

¼ tsp. garlic powder

¼ tsp. dried thyme

1 cup couscous

TOOLS

1-qt. (1L) sauce pot

Lid or aluminum foil

Serving spoon

1 Combine the stock and seasonings in the sauce pot. Bring to a boil over high heat (fig. a).

2 Mix in the couscous and immediately turn off the flame (fig. b).

3 Remove the pot from the stove and cover with a lid or aluminum foil (fig. c). Allow the couscous to steep for 5 minutes.

4 Remove the lid and fluff the couscous with the serving spoon. Serve immediately hot, or allow it to cool and serve as a salad.

 Chef's Note

Couscous is generally thought of as a Middle Eastern dish, although it has been eaten throughout the world since the fifteenth century. In fact, in a 2011 poll, the French rated it the third most popular dish in their country.

potatoes and beans

In this chapter, you'll learn the fundamentals of buying, storing, and cooking potatoes and beans. The essential skills of roasting, boiling, and pressure cooking starches are shown in the recipes. In addition, you'll learn the complexities of different types of potatoes and the wide variety of uses for beans.

Potato Basics

Potatoes are a major part of the caloric intake for a large portion of the world's population, however their popularity is relatively recent, as potatoes were discovered in North America and taken to Europe in the eighteenth century. It wasn't until the latter part of the century that a nutritionist named Antoine-Augustin Parmentier made potatoes popular.

There are thousands of varieties of potatoes, but they typically are classified in two general categories: *starchy* and *waxy*. When you cook potatoes, you have to think about which category of potato is best suited for the dish and the cooking method.

Starchy potatoes are lower in moisture content. The typical varieties you hear about in this category are russets and Idaho. They're elongated and usually larger than waxy potatoes, and tend to have a rough skin. If the potato is particularly gnarly and rough, it's referred to as a *chef potato*.

Waxy potatoes are high in moisture and also higher in sugars. They tend to be rounder and smoother skinned, and their flesh can be many different colors—white, yellow, blue, and even purple. Because of their high sugar content, care must be taken when you cook them. For example, deep frying these potatoes will cause dark streaks, which are a result of their higher sugar content.

Buying

When you purchase potatoes, look for smooth and firm fruit. Avoid shriveled or spongy potatoes, as well as any that are green or have started to sprout. Also check for black or soft spots, which are signs of rotting.

Storing

Store potatoes in a cool, dry, dark place, ideally 55° to 60°F (13° to 16°C). They store well if you have a basement. If not, a closet on an exterior wall is a good place to turn into a food pantry.

Don't store potatoes at temperatures below 45°F (7°C), because this will turn the starches into sugars. If this does happen, you can change them back to starches by placing them in a warmer environment for two weeks. Also, don't store potatoes in sunlight, as the light causes them to form a green skin. The green spots are very bitter and slightly poisonous.

When a potato is peeled or cut, the exposed flesh will quickly become brown due to oxidization. To keep this from happening, store peeled potatoes in cool water. They can be kept in the water for up to four hours. But remember, if you store potatoes in water below 45°F (7°C), sugars will develop and you'll start to lose the starch.

4

 5 minutes

 45 minutes

INGREDIENTS

4 Idaho-style potatoes,
  about 8 oz. (225g) each

4 TB. vegetable oil

2 TB. kosher salt

4 tsp. butter

TOOLS

Potato brush

Sheet pan

Paring knife

Baked Potatoes

Baking potatoes is a fundamental cooking skill. The important things to remember are to oil the potato before cooking, salt the outside, and don't cover them with foil, as this will hold in moisture and result in soggy skin instead of a crispy skin. The process is the same for making a baked sweet potato as well.

1 Preheat the oven to 350°F (120°C). Under cold running water, brush the dirt off of the potatoes and dry them with a paper towel (fig. a).

2 Place the potatoes on a sheet pan and rub them with vegetable oil (fig. b).

3 Salt the exterior of the potatoes (fig. c). This allows the heat to evenly cook the potato and the moisture to stay in without just steaming the potato. You'll get a more flavorful potato with a crunchy skin.

4 Bake for 45 minutes and check for doneness by sticking a paring knife in the largest potato (fig. d). If you feel resistance in the middle, allow to cook for 10 minutes longer. If the knife goes cleanly into the potato, remove from the oven and allow to rest for 5 minutes before serving.

5 Cut a slit in the top of each potato and add a teaspoon of butter (fig. e).

POTATOES AND BEANS

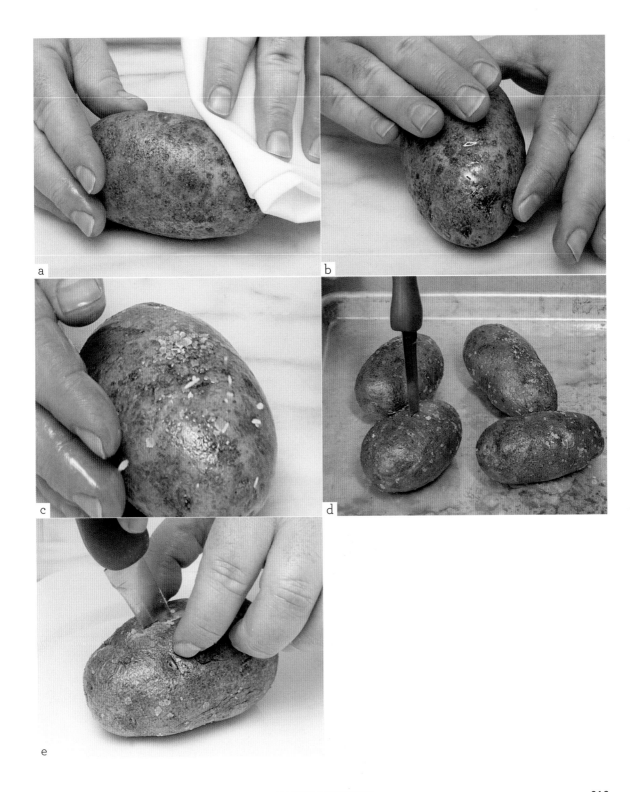

Roasted Red Potatoes

Roasted potatoes are a winter staple in many households. The pleasing aroma of the rosemary in this dish will fill the house and remind you of a cool autumn day. These potatoes are a perfect accompaniment to hearty stewed dishes.

 4

 15 minutes

20 minutes

INGREDIENTS

10 small red potatoes

1 tsp. kosher salt

½ tsp. black pepper

1 tsp. fresh rosemary leaves, chopped

4 TB. vegetable oil

TOOLS

Mixing bowl

Sheet pan

Serving platter

Chef's knife

a

1 Preheat the oven to 400°F (120°C). Cut the potatoes in half (fig. a) and then dice them.

2 Put the potatoes in a bowl and mix them with salt, pepper, and rosemary. Add the oil to the mix and evenly coat all the potatoes (fig. b).

b

3 Place the potatoes on a sheet pan with the cut side facing up (fig. c). Roast the potatoes in the oven for 20 minutes or until golden brown.

Serve as a side dish, or put on a platter and serve family style. Add a fresh sprig of rosemary on top of the potatoes, and the aroma will enhance the dish when served.

c

 Essential Technique: Roasting Starches

Starches such as potatoes, beans, and rice all convert to sugars with heat and moisture, and sugars will burn if they're left in a dry heat, so it's important to keep a close eye on starches when you cook them. Once the moisture in the food has reduced, you'll start to see browning. This is the point where it can go from brown to burn in a matter of minutes.

4

 15 minutes

20 minutes

INGREDIENTS

1 lb. (450g) Idaho
  potatoes

1 lb. (450g) Yukon gold
  potatoes

½ gal. cold water

2 TB. kosher salt

½ cup heavy cream

2 TB. butter

TOOLS

Scale

Potato brush

Potato peeler

Paring knife

1-gal. pot

Strainer

Small pot

Mixing bowl

Potato masher

Mashed Potatoes

Boiling potatoes bump into each other and the sides of the pot causing corners to break off, especially if the potatoes are high in starch. If you boil a creamy white potato, it disintegrates after 30 minutes, but a mealy Idaho will hold up.

1 Under running water, brush the dirt off the potatoes. Peel and cut out any bad spots. Cut the potatoes into pieces about 1½ inches (5cm) in size (fig. a). Place the potatoes in a pot of cold water. They'll start to turn brown if not kept in water after they're peeled and/or cut.

2 Put the pot on the stove over high heat. Bring the water to a boil and cook for 20 minutes. Check for doneness by sticking a paring knife in the largest piece of potato. If you feel resistance in the middle, allow to cook 5 minutes longer. When the knife goes cleanly into the potato, remove from the stove and drain the water immediately (fig. b).

3 In a small pot, combine salt, cream, and butter. Heat over a medium flame until the butter is melted (fig. c).

4 After the potatoes have drained and while still hot, put them into a mixing bowl (fig. d). Pour in the cream mixture (fig. e). Using the potato masher, start pressing through the potatoes. Continue until potatoes are smooth and creamy (fig. f).

Serve as a side dish on a plate, or family style in a large serving bowl.

 Mashed, Smashed, and Whipped
What's the difference between the styles of creamed potatoes?

Mashed potatoes are peeled, boiled, and hand pulverized with a ricer, food mill, or potato masher. *Smashed* potatoes aren't peeled, they're boiled and then pulverized with a potato masher. *Whipped potatoes* are peeled, boiled, and pulverized using a mixer. (Be careful using this method—if they're over-mixed, the starches will become gummy.)

Bean Basics

Beans belong to a family of legumes called *pulses*. These are plants that have double-seamed pods with a single row of seeds inside. This is the same general family of plants as green beans; the difference is that the pods of pulses dry and the seeds inside are used as dried beans. Pulses include hundreds of different types of beans—from pinto and black beans to lentils and soybeans.

Beans are an important protein source for a large portion of the world's population. In fact, when beans are consumed with a grain, they form a complete protein. Beans are 20 to 25 percent fat, are high in vitamins and minerals, and have no cholesterol.

Purchasing

Beans can be purchased canned or dried. The canned varieties don't require soaking before use, but also don't tend to have the same depth of flavor as dried beans. When buying dried beans, look for beans that are dust and mold free. They should be bright and have a bit of shine to them.

Storing

Store canned beans in a cool place away from direct sunlight. You should store dried beans in an air-tight container so they don't absorb moisture from the air. Use within six months of purchasing for best flavor.

Cooking

Before cooking either dried or canned beans, be sure to rinse them. With dried beans, remove any loose skins and look for any tiny pebbles left after picking and packaging. Most dried beans should be soaked in water overnight before cooking to make them easier to digest.

Most beans can be used interchangeably in recipes, depending on your taste.

Variations

Many variations of hummus have started appearing in gourmet food stores. These variations use the base recipe and then add a flavor element.

Roasted red pepper hummus: Add 1 roasted red pepper to the food processor.

Guacamole hummus: Add the flesh of 1 avocado to the food processor.

Sun-dried tomato and basil hummus: Purée in 5 sun-dried tomatoes and 5 basil leaves.

Bacon hummus: Cook 5 slices of bacon and purée into the base recipe.

Use your imagination to create your own.

Hummus

Hummus is made from chickpeas, a pulse with two seeds in the shell. In India, *hummus* is actually the word for "chickpea." In India, the pulse is ground with tahini to make this luscious dip. It's easy to make with a food processor.

 10

 5 minutes

 none

INGREDIENTS

1½ cups canned chick-peas, drained

¼ cup tahini (sesame paste)

3 garlic cloves, peeled

1 oz. (225mL) lemon juice

2 oz. (450mL) olive oil

1 tsp. kosher salt

¼ tsp. cayenne pepper

TOOLS

Food processor

Serving spoon

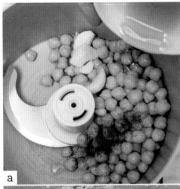

a

b

1 Combine all ingredients in the food processor (fig. a).

2 Run the food processor until all the ingredients are smooth and emulsified (fig. b).

3 Taste the paste and adjust the salt and pepper as needed. Pour into a serving bowl. Serve with pita bread.

4

 5 minutes +
overnight

 1 hour

INGREDIENTS

1 cup great northern
 beans, dried

3 cups cold water

3 cups chicken stock

3 TB. olive oil

10 leaves sage, whole,
 fresh

3 garlic cloves, chopped

1 TB. kosher salt

TOOLS

Bowl for soaking

Strainer

2-qt. (2L) sauce pot

Lid or aluminum foil

Serving spoon

Serving platter

Tuscan White Beans

Cooking dried beans is a two-step process: first you rehydrate them by soaking in cold water overnight, then drain the water and cook the beans. The soaking process dissolves the indigestible starch that gives some people gas.

1 Put the beans in a bowl and cover with cold water at least 2 inches (5cm) over the top of the beans. Allow the bowl to sit overnight to rehydrate the beans (fig. a).

2 The next day, strain the beans out of the bowl and discard the water. Put the beans in a pot with the rest of the ingredients (fig. b).

3 Bring the mixture up to a boil and then turn down to a slow simmer (fig. c). Simmer the beans covered for 1 hour.

4 Taste a bean for doneness. If the center is still crunchy, continue to cook. If the liquid in the pot runs low, add more water. When the beans are cooked through, serve hot, or cool quickly.

a

b

c

TUSCAN WHITE BEANS

POTATOES AND BEANS

Black Beans and Rice

This dish uses two recipes: the rice pilaf in the Pastas and Grains chapter is combined with black beans to make a complete protein. This marriage has been the main protein source for many cultures for the past couple of centuries.

 8

 5 minutes + overnight

 22 minutes

INGREDIENTS

1½ cups cooked rice pilaf

1 cup black beans, dried

3 cups cold water

3 cups beef stock

3 TB. olive oil (bacon fat can also be used)

3 garlic cloves, chopped

1 TB. kosher salt

TOOLS

Bowl for soaking

Strainer

2-qt. (2L) pressure cooker

Serving spoon

Serving platter

1 Put the beans in a bowl and cover with cold water at least 2 inches (5cm) over the top of the beans (fig. a). Allow the bowl to sit overnight to rehydrate the beans.

2 The next day, strain the beans out of the bowl and discard the water. Put the beans in a pressure cooker with the rest of the ingredients (fig. b). Bring the cooker up to a simmer at 5 to 10 atmospheres of pressure using the manufacturer's directions. Simmer the beans for 20 minutes.

3 Open the pressure cooker per the manufacturer's directions (fig. c). Taste the beans for doneness and flavor.

4 Put the rice on the serving platter as a base. Spoon the beans into the middle of the rice (fig. d). Serve the platter as a side dish or as an entrée.

fruits and vegetables

In this chapter, you'll learn the fundamentals of fruits, vegetables, and mushrooms. The essential skills of *steaming*, *blanching* and *shocking*, and cooking liquids *au sec* will be shown in the recipes. In addition, you'll learn how to treat green and red vegetables in ways that help maintain their bright colors.

Fruits and Vegetables 101

There are many different theories when it comes to growing foods. Some are strongly debated between farmers and even between countries. As a consumer, you should be aware how your food is grown or raised—it could have a direct impact on the flavor and nutrition of the food. Here are some terms you should know:

Conventional agriculture is the most prevalent way of growing a particular food. This means the crops and fields are commonly sprayed with chemicals such as fertilizers, herbicides, pesticides, fungicides, and chemicals to enhance ripening. These help produce a consistent crop that's free of blemishes.

A *genetically modified organism (GMO)* is a seed that has been modified so it strengthens different characteristics. This could mean that a salmon gene is spliced onto a corn seed to help the corn stay sweet in transport. Or the seed is modified to help with pest resistance so the farmer doesn't have to use more chemicals. GMOs are regulated in many countries, but before using GMO products, make sure you understand their impacts on flavor and health and beware that GMOs don't have to be labeled as such. Ask your grocer or farmer about the product you buy.

Sustainable agricultural practices are used by many smaller farmers and it means they try to promote environmental stewardship. They use practices that keep the soil fertile, minimize soil erosion, and promote beneficial co-planting. This isn't governed, so ask the farmers what sustainable means to them.

Organic farming is governed by government-sanctioned third parties. In organic farming, all the inputs used adhere to "natural" practices. This means farmers cannot use some of the items that conventional agriculture uses, such as synthetic fertilizers, sewage sludge, bioengineering, GMOs, and ionizing radiation.

Ionizing radiation is the practice of killing pathogens on fruits and vegetables by using low amounts of radiation in the processing. Labeling is not required for this practice, so be sure to ask your grocer if the product has been radiated.

Seasonality used to be very important. However, with modern shipping methods, GMO seeds, and radiation, most fruits and vegetables are now available year-round. Beware that just because corn is available at the store in January doesn't mean you should eat it. After fruits and vegetables are picked, they begin to lose their nutrients, so if products take eight weeks to get to the market, they have lost a substantial amount of their benefits (and flavor). If you can buy local food that's in season and picked within the week, you'll get much higher nutritional value and, more than likely, better flavor.

Locally grown is a term that's hard to define, depending on how many miles actually defines local. It's generally understood that if the farmer could reasonably pick the food and deliver it to you within the same workday, it's locally grown. Many times with locally grown food you can meet the grower and ask about their growing practices. You can also often get specialty fruits and vegetables that wouldn't withstand longer journeys. Moreover, spending money locally increases the economy of your area.

Fruit Basics

Fruits are the ovaries that surround or contain seeds. They are generally categorized as tree fruit, berries, citrus, grapes, melons, stone fruits, and "others."

Purchasing

When you purchase fruits, look for items that are free of bruising, mold, and soft spots. Also look for nice plump fruits, not shriveled ones. The grocer should not have fruits under refrigeration unless they're fully mature.

If you're going to be cutting up the fruit or puréeing it, look for fruit "seconds"—these are fruits that might not be perfectly shaped or that have marks on them. Since you won't be eating or serving them whole, these marks don't make any difference, and they're usually sold at a significantly lower price.

Storing

In most cases, store fruit at 40° to 45°F (4.5° to 7°C) with 80 to 90 percent humidity. The exception is bananas, which should be stored at room temperature. If the fruit is not totally mature, store it at 65° to 70°F (18° to 20°C) until it's ripe, then move it to the refrigerator.

Many varieties of apples store for up to 10 months. You can keep them in a plastic bag that has holes in it, which allows moisture to stay in the bag. Put them in a crisper drawer in the refrigerator.

All fruits should be stored whole, stem on and not washed. Once the item is washed or rinsed it will start to grow molds and bacteria.

Strawberries, raspberries, and blueberries can be frozen whole without any processing. You can put the whole, unwashed berries in the freezer in their containers. They'll become soft, but they're still wonderful for baking, adding to smoothies, or mixing into yogurt.

Chef's Tip

Most family orchards have a market store, which is a great place to get your apples and other tree fruit in the fall. Most also carry other fruits and vegetables that were grown by local farmers. I go to the orchard store to get informed about what's in season during the entire growing year.

10

 15 minutes

 10 minutes

INGREDIENTS

1 cup almonds, toasted

1 cup mini-marshmallows

1 cup amaretto

1 pineapple, peeled, cored, diced (see following spread)

2 oranges, seeded and segmented

1 qt. (225g) strawberries, stemmed and cut in half

TOOLS

Sheet pan

1-qt. (1L) saucepan

Mixing bowl

Serving spoon

Serving bowl

Fruit Salad

Fruit salad makes a great dessert on a hot day. It's light and refreshing, making for a clean palate. Pay close attention to your knife skills when preparing this salad; people will take notice of the colors and shapes of the fruit.

1 Preheat the oven to 300°F (144°C). Spread the almonds on a sheet pan (fig. a). Place in the preheated oven for 5 minutes to toast. Remove from the oven and reserve at room temperature.

2 Combine the amaretto and marshmallows in a small saucepan (fig. b). Put them on the stove at medium heat. Mix until all the marshmallows melt (fig. c). Remove from the stove and hold at room temperature.

3 In a mixing bowl, combine all the fruit. Top with the toasted nuts (fig. d)

4 Pour the amaretto-marshmallow sauce over the top. Mix the fruit salad together (fig. e) and place in a serving bowl.

Cutting a Pineapple

Fresh pineapple is much better in flavor than canned pineapple. It's easy to cut once you know how.

1. Cut the green top off ½ inch (1.25cm) below where it meets the fruit (fig. a).

2. Cut the base off ½ inch (1.25cm) from the bottom.

3. Peel the outside off in strips, going just below the eye's depth (fig. b).

4. Cut across the pineapple straight down where you see the texture of the pineapple change to the hard center (fig. c). Continue to do this around the core until the flesh has been removed from the core (fig. d).

5. Discard the core, peels, top, and bottom.

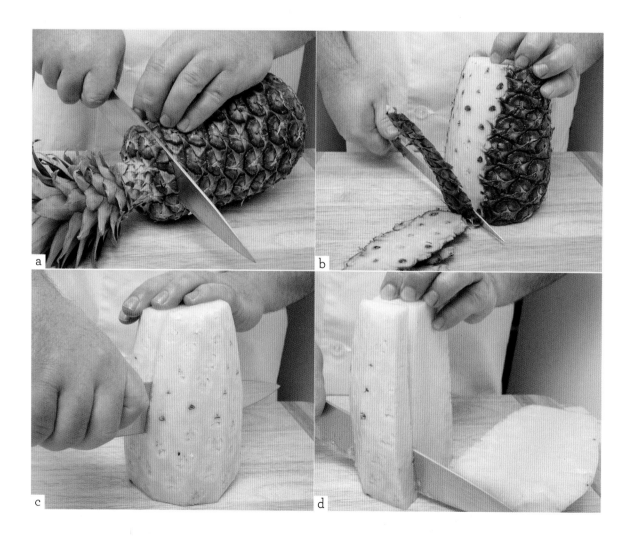

Variations

Digestive health: banana, yogurt, honey, grated ginger

Muscle soreness: Orange, fat-free dairy, vanilla extract, ice

Antioxidant: 4 ounces (120mL) green tea, honey, blueberries, banana, hemp milk

Fiber boost: Apple juice, banana, kiwi, strawberries, honey

Vitamin C boost: Apricot, mango, yogurt, lemon juice, vanilla extract, ice

Energy boost: Strawberry, blueberry, raspberry, honey, lemon juice, ice

Immunity boost: Pineapple, yogurt, mango, banana, ice

Detoxification: Raspberries, rice milk, cherries, honey, ginger, flaxseed, lemon juice

Superfood detox: Kale, mango, celery, orange, parsley, mint

Fruit Smoothie

Smoothies are a common breakfast for people on the go because they're quick and easy to make. Just put the ingredients together in a food processor and purée. Health benefits will vary according to the mix of fruits and vegetables you use.

 2

 10 minutes

 none

INGREDIENTS

1 cup blueberries

1 peach, cut in half, pit removed

1 banana, peeled, cut into pieces

1 cup coconut milk

TOOLS

Blender

Serving cups

1. Combine all ingredients in a blender.

2. Blend on high until smooth.

3. Pour into glasses and serve.

Chef's Tip

Look for freestone varieties when buying peaches. The pit will easily come out of these peaches. Clingstone varieties are more suited for eating out of hand, as the pit is very hard to cut out.

Chef's Note

Peaches were originally cultivated in China as early as 1000 B.C.E. The peach is a sacred plant in China, a symbol of immortality and unity. Chinese brides carry peach blossoms as a sign of unity.

Vegetable Basics

Vegetables are the roots, leaves, stems, or flower heads of plants that are safe for human consumption. In some cases, such as tomatoes, fruits are put into the vegetable category based on their culinary uses.

Purchasing

When you purchase vegetables, look for items that are free of bruising, mold, and soft spots. They should be stored in a 40° to 45°F (4.5° to 7°C) area at the grocer's unless they contain a seed. Vegetables with seeds may be left out in the market.

Storing

In most cases, store vegetables at 40° to 45°F (4.5° to 7°C) with 80 to 90 percent humidity. The exception is tomatoes, potatoes, and dry onions, which should be stored at room temperature.

All vegetables should be stored whole, stem on, and not washed. Once the item is washed or rinsed, it will start to grow molds and bacteria.

 Chef's Note

When working with vegetables, it's important to understand how the colors react to acids and alkalis. Vegetables are considered to have one of three colors as their base color:

The green color in a plant is from chlorophyll. When chlorophyll comes in contact with an acid, it turns brown. When it comes in contact with an alkali, it makes the green color brighter.

Red color comes from flavonoids. These are strengthened by acids and turn bluer from alkalis.

Carotenoids are mainly orange. These are not affected by pH.

FRUITS AND VEGETABLES

Steamed Broccoli

 4

 15 minutes

 8 minutes

While the basic technique of steaming vegetables is straightforward, there are nuances. Green vegetables don't like acid, which turns them brown. Time is important—the longer the green vegetable is in the steamer, the more acidic the water becomes, so pulling the broccoli out before it overcooks is very important.

INGREDIENTS

2 lb. (1kg) broccoli, stemmed and cut

1 tsp. sea salt

¼ tsp. white pepper

1 tsp. extra virgin olive oil

1 Steam the broccoli for 5 minutes (figs. a and b) following the directions below in How to Steam Vegetables.

2 Remove from the steamer and rinse in cold water for 1 minute to set the color (fig. c).

3 Toss in a mixing bowl with salt, pepper, and olive oil (fig. d).

TOOLS

Steamer

Mixing bowl

Serving spoon

Serving bowl

 How to Steam Vegetables

Steaming vegetables is one of the healthiest ways to cook them. It's a straightforward process that's the same no matter what vegetable you're making.

1. Make sure the vegetable is cut to similar-size pieces.

2. Put about 1 inch (2.5cm) of water in the bottom of your steamer pan.

3. Bring the water to a boil.

4. Add the steamer basket with the vegetables.

5. Cover and cook to desired doneness.

8

 15 minutes

 40 minutes

INGREDIENTS

5 small red potatoes, cut
in half

3 carrots, peeled and
cut into 1-inch (2.5cm)
pieces

10 radishes, stem and
root end trimmed

1 onion, large diced

1 tsp. kosher salt

½ tsp. black pepper

1 tsp. fresh thyme leaves

2 cloves garlic, minced

4 TB. vegetable oil

TOOLS

Mixing bowl

Sheet pan

Serving spoon

Serving platter

Roasted Winter Root Vegetables

Roasting root vegetables is a great way to accent their deep flavors. It's important that all the vegetables are of similar size and the same firmness.

1 Preheat the oven to 300°F (188°C). Put the vegetables in a bowl and mix them with salt, pepper, thyme, and the garlic (fig. a).

2 Add the oil to the mix and evenly coat all the ingredients (fig. b).

3 Place the mixture on a sheet pan. Roast in the oven for 40 minutes or until golden brown.

4 Put the vegetables in a serving bowl and serve with an entrée.

a

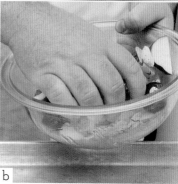
b

 Chef's Tip

There are many varieties and colors of carrots. They come in red, purple, orange, and white, and it looks interesting on the plate if you can serve a variety of colors. Serving different colors also helps provide a larger variety of nutrients in the dish.

What Are Root Vegetables?

Root vegetables are a large group that also includes tubers. The sub-
categories include beets, carrots, celery root, chokes, jicama, parsnips,
radishes, and turnips. Although they have their own taste qualities,
they can all be used interchangeably in most recipes.

Chef's Tip

Chef's Tip

As summer squash grow larger they develop seeds through the middle, and the larger they get, the more bitterness that will be created from seed development, so steer clear of larger summer squash.

Grilled Summer Squash

This summer squash recipe is so simple, yet it will make everyone happy—from family members to gourmands. Summer squash brings out the flavors of whatever it's cooked with, so start with good quality ingredients.

 4

 2 minutes

 8 minutes

INGREDIENTS

2 zucchini, no longer than 6 inches (15cm)

2 yellow squash, no longer than 6 inches (15cm)

1 TB. kosher salt

1 tsp. black pepper

2 cloves garlic, minced

Pan spray

2 TB. balsamic vinegar

4 leaves fresh basil, chopped

TOOLS

Tongs

Transport tray

Serving platter

Serving plates

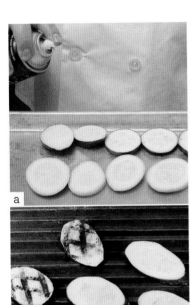

1 Start the grill for medium-high direct-heat cooking. Remove the stem end and bloom end of the squash and cut into thin slices from end to end. Salt and pepper the slices, sprinkle with minced garlic, and spray with pan spray (fig. a).

2 Place the squash on the grill (fig. b). After 2 minutes, rotate 90 degrees to form a cross-hatch pattern. After 2 more minutes, flip and repeat the process on the other side.

3 Remove to a serving platter. Drizzle with balsamic vinegar (fig. c). Sprinkle basil on top.

 A Summer Abundance

Anyone who has grown summer squash in their garden knows the plants can be very prolific, and many gardeners try to give them away because they can't keep up with the plants. I grew up in the country, and the only time we locked our doors was during zucchini season. We were afraid the neighbors would come in and leave us a table full of the squash!

4

 5 minutes

 16 minutes

INGREDIENTS

2 lbs. green beans, stems removed

Ice water as needed

1 tsp. sea salt

½ tsp. white pepper

1 tsp. extra virgin olive oil

TOOLS

2-qt. (2L) pot

Mixing bowl

Large sauté pan

Serving spoon

Serving bowl

Sautéed Green Beans

Green beans are a classic summer vegetable. They're often even used on main courses year-around because of their ability to freeze and can well. We capture green beans' bright summer flavors in this recipe.

1 Bring a pot of water up to a boil. Put the green beans in the boiling water and bring down to a simmer for 3 minutes (fig. a).

2 Remove the beans from the water and immediately put them in a bowl of ice water to stop the cooking and set the color (fig. b).

3 When time to serve, toss in a hot sauté pan with salt, pepper, and olive oil. Sauté the green beans for 4 minutes, or until heated through (fig. c).

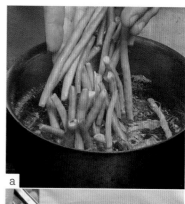
a

b

c

Essential Technique: Blanching and Shocking

Most vegetables that are going to be sautéed need to be cooked first. The process of blanching is similar to steaming, but instead you completely submerge the vegetables in simmering water to cook them, and then plunge them into ice water to stop the cooking at just the right time. At this point, they can be held until it's time to serve them. Just use the sauté method to finish them in the sauté pan.

Differences with Green Cabbage

This recipe also works well with green cabbage. The main difference in the cooking is the acids need to be replaced by alkalis, because you want to keep the green color in green cabbage. So, don't use vinegar when cooking green cabbage; instead, add 1 teaspoon of baking soda to the recipe in place of the apple cider vinegar.

Braised Red Cabbage

 8

 15 minutes

 35 minutes

Braised cabbage is a dish most people might turn their nose up to at first. The thought of the strong smell of cabbage cooking makes them want to avoid it at all costs. But when it's cooked for a shorter time, the unpleasant odors are not produced.

INGREDIENTS

1 head red cabbage, cut very thin

6 slices bacon, small diced

¼ cup vegetable oil

1 onion, small diced

1 TB. kosher salt

1 tsp. black pepper

½ cup red wine

½ cup chicken stock

¼ tsp. ground cinnamon

2 Granny Smith apples, medium diced

1 TB. brown sugar

2 TB. apple cider vinegar

TOOLS

Apple corer or chef's knife

Large sauté pan

Lid or aluminum foil

Mixing bowl

Serving spoon

Serving platter

a

b

c

1 Put the bacon in the pan with the vegetable oil on high heat and cook until crisp. Add the onions and cook until translucent (fig. a). Add the cabbage and cook 5 minutes.

2 Add the salt, pepper, wine, stock, and cinnamon to the pan (fig. b). Once the liquids boil, turn down to a simmer and cover for 20 minutes or until the cabbage is tender.

3 Add the apples, sugar, and vinegar (fig. c). Mix until the vinegar is evenly distributed. Notice how the red color comes back to the cabbage from the acid in the vinegar. Allow to simmer 5 more minutes, uncovered this time.

4 Remove the cabbage from the pan to a serving bowl. Serve as a side dish for full-flavored meats.

Mushroom Basics

Mushrooms are fungi that don't technically belong in the vegetable category, but are commonly accepted as a vegetable. There are thousands of varieties of mushrooms, many of which are poisonous, so make sure you only buy mushrooms from a certified seller.

Mushrooms can be purchased as *fresh cultivate*, meaning that they're grown for the purpose of making food out of them. This category would include white button, cremini, portobello (adult cremini), shiitake, and oyster mushrooms. You can also buy wild mushrooms, which grow in the wild and are often foraged by some people. This is the category where it's imperative that you purchase from a certified seller. There are many poisonous types that look like edible mushrooms, and a minor mistake could be a deadly one.

How to Buy

When purchasing mushrooms from the grocer, make sure they're whole and firm. They shouldn't show any signs of deterioration, chipping, or breaking. All of these could be signs of older age and the development of bad toxins.

If you're buying wild mushrooms from a market, ask the seller to see certification that the mushrooms are safe for human consumption.

Storage

Store mushrooms in the refrigerator in an open container in a single layer. Don't wash or cut until you're ready to use them.

 Chef's Tip

Dried mushrooms are readily available in the off-seasons. Just 3 ounces (85g) of a dried mushroom will be equal to 1 pound when reconstituted. If you use dried mushrooms, cover them with water and allow them to sit for four hours to reconstitute. Then use as you would fresh mushrooms in the recipe. Remember, though, dried will never have the same quality taste as fresh.

How to Prepare

Brush fresh mushrooms with a cloth and remove any hard or dirty stems. Mushrooms are sponges, so if you submerge them in water you'll end up with a soggy mess. If you cook mushrooms in aluminum foil, they'll turn black. And never cook mushrooms if they show any signs of decay—they harbor toxins as they go bad.

4

 15 minutes

 40 minutes

INGREDIENTS

2 lbs. (1kg) mushrooms, chopped (this seems like a ton, but it isn't when cooked down)

1 onion, fine chopped

3 cloves garlic, minced

¼ cup vegetable oil

TOOLS

Large sauté pan

Storage container

Metal tongs

Mushroom Duxelles

Mushroom Duxelles can be made ahead of time and kept to enhance the flavor of other dishes. If you cook a meat dish and think, "This is missing something!", toss in a spoonful of this and make your dish pop with rich flavor.

1 Put the sauté pan with oil on high heat. Once the oil is hot, add the mushrooms (fig. a). You may have to add in batches if they won't all fit in the pan. As they start to cook, you'll see the water start coming out of the mushrooms. Continue to cook on high heat until all water has disappeared out of the pan.

2 Add the onions and garlic and continue to cook until the onions are translucent (fig. b).

3 Remove from the pan to a storage container. Store in the refrigerator until needed.

 Essential Technique: Cooking Au Sec

Au sec means "almost dry." If you let liquids simmer down, all the moisture will eventually evaporate away. This is the way you concentrate flavors. When you cook mushrooms, the moisture will be purged, and by simmering until they're au sec, you get a more concentrated mushroom flavor.

a

b

MUSHROOM DUXELLES 253

Sausage Stuffed Mushroom Caps

Stuffed mushroom caps make great hors d'ouevres or even a breakfast accompaniment. You can prepare large batches ahead of time and freeze before they're fully cooked, and you'll only need to pull them from the freezer and cook for the final 40 minutes.

 5

 15 minutes

 50 minutes

INGREDIENTS

1 lb. (450g) Italian sausage

½ cup ricotta cheese

½ cup Mushroom Duxelles

1 cup dried breadcrumbs

20 large button mushrooms, stems removed

½ cup Parmesan cheese, grated

TOOLS

Large sauté pan

Sheet pan

Wooden spoon

Serving platter

a

b

1 Preheat the oven to 300°F (148°C). Cook the sausage in a large sauté pan over high heat until it's fully browned. Crumble the sausage with the back of a wooden spoon when you first add it to the pan.

2 Turn off the flame. Add the ricotta and Mushroom Duxelles to the pan and mix completely (fig. a). Add the breadcrumbs and again fully combine all ingredients.

3 Stuff the sausage filling into the cavities of the mushrooms and place them on a sheet pan (fig. b). After they're completely stuffed, top them with grated Parmesan and place them in the oven for 40 minutes. Serve hot.

4

 20 minutes

 8 minutes

INGREDIENTS

2 garlic cloves, peeled, chopped

3 TB. balsamic vinegar

2 TB. lemon juice

1 TB. dark soy sauce

½ cup red wine

1 tsp. dried basil

¼ tsp. black pepper

4 portobello mushrooms

Pan spray

4 TB. bleu cheese

4 hamburger buns

TOOLS

Mixing bowl

Whisk

Soup spoon

Transport tray

Tongs

Serving platter

Portobello Mushroom Sandwich

For many years chefs turned to portobello mushrooms whenever they were serving a vegetarian meal. These mushrooms are big and have a full flavor. They'll leave you full and happy, and best of all, they're quick and easy to fix.

1 In a mixing bowl, whisk together garlic, balsamic vinegar, lemon juice, soy sauce, red wine, basil, and pepper. Remove stems from the mushrooms by carefully holding the cap at the base of the stem in one hand, and pulling off the stem with the other (fig. a). Place the caps on the tray gill side up. Sprinkle the whisked marinade into the caps and allow them to sit for at least 20 minutes (fig. b).

2 Start the grill for medium-high direct heat cooking. Pour any marinade left in the caps back into the mixing bowl. Spray both sides of the caps with pan spray. Place the caps on direct heat, cap side down. Allow to cook for 4 minutes.

3 With the tongs, carefully lift the caps and pour the accumulated liquid into the mixing bowl with the marinade. Put the caps back on the grill with the gill side down (fig. c). Allow to cook an additional 4 minutes.

4 Turn the caps over and pour the marinade mixture back into them. Top with bleu cheese (fig. d). Allow to cook with the lid closed for 4 minutes.

5 Remove from the grill to the hamburger buns and serve.

 You could use this recipe to cook most varieties of mushrooms. With the smaller species you can toss them in a grill basket so they don't fall through the grates. Many people don't know portobello mushrooms are the adult version of cremini. When a cremini mushroom gets larger than 4 inches (10cm), it's categorized as a portobello.

PORTOBELLO MUSHROOM SANDWICH   257

Index